## Disclaimer

*Recipes were submitted by preppers from all over America - this cookbook is dedicated to them. To the best of my knowledge, all recipes are original or otherwise in the public domain.*

# TABLE OF CONTENTS

## CHAPTER 1: STOCKING THE BASICS

Most food storage recommendations are based on the LDS Church's booklet, *Essentials of Home Production and Storage*. I agree with this approach and recommend that you start with the basics: wheat, rice, beans, cornmeal, oatmeal, salt and powdered milk. It is imperative that you include yeast and baking soda, as these are essential ingredients in making bread. Some kind of fat (shortening or vegetable oil) is also important. Some form of sugar, although not essential, will certainly be appreciated. Either white sugar or honey will work, as these sugars have a very long storage life, if stored properly.

In this brief chapter, we examine each basic category of food and list the recommend amounts. We also indicate what can be made with that staple.

### Grains

Grains are the bread of life. This category includes wheat, rice and corn. Below are the recommended amounts per person.

| | |
|---|---|
| Wheat | 150 lbs. |
| Rice | 50 lbs. |
| Flour | 25 lbs. |
| Cornmeal | 25 lbs. |
| Oatmeal | 25 lbs. |
| Pasta | 25 lbs. |
| | 600 lbs. |

This may sound like a lot of food. But this represents only the basic minimum necessary to survive.

With these grains, you will be able to make wheat gruel, corn gruel, rice, plain oatmeal and dry pasta. Such meals will provide nutrition, but not complete nutrition.

### Fats and Oils

Fats and oils are calorie dense. They provide essential flavoring for foods. Without fats and oils, you cannot bake wheat into bread.

| | |
|---|---|
| Shortening | 4 lbs. |
| Vegetable Oil | 2 gal. |
| Peanut Butter | 4 lbs. |
| Salad Dressing | 1 qt. |
| | 13 lbs. |

Notice that 13 lbs. of fats and oils (per person) will give you the capability of baking breads. At this point, we have not added yeast or baking soda, so the breads that can be made are limited to flat breads and tortillas.

## Cooking Essentials

| | |
|---|---|
| Baking Powder | 1 lb. |
| Baking Soda | 1 lb. |
| Yeast | 1 lb. |
| Salt | 5 lbs. |
| Vinegar | <u>1 gal.</u> |
| | 9 lbs. |

We have now added 9 lbs. of basic cooking supplies. With the addition of these supplies, you will now able to make a wide range of breads.

## Legumes

| | |
|---|---|
| Dry Beans | 30 lbs. |
| Lima Beans | 5 lbs. |
| Soy Beans | 10 lbs. |
| Split Peas | 5 lbs. |
| Lentils | 5 lbs. |
| Dry Soup Mix | <u>5 lbs.</u> |
| | 60 lbs. |

Dry beans are an excellent source of protein. You will also be able to grow bean sprouts. This will provide Vitamin C. (Most shelf stable foods lack this essential nutrient.)  At this point in our culinary adventure, you can make a complete meal, beans and rice with whole wheat bread. If this were all you had to eat for weeks at a time, you would soon grow tired of beans and rice.

## Sugars

| | |
|---|---|
| Honey | 3 lbs. |
| Sugar | 40 lbs. |
| Brown sugar | 3 lbs. |
| Molasses | 1 lb. |
| Corn syrup | 3 lbs. |
| Jams | 3 lbs. |
| Drink Powder | 6 lbs. |
| Flavored gelatin | <u>1 lb.</u> |
| | 60 lbs. |

Note, once again, that this list represents a bare minimum. If you are baking bread everyday, you will certainly want more honey and jam to spread on the bread. If you are canning, you certainly need significantly more sugar, salt and vinegar. (Note: If you plan on canning your own foods, be sure to include both table salt and canning salt.)

**Dairy**

| | |
|---|---|
| Milk Powder | 60 lbs. |
| Evaporated milk | 12 cans |
| Other | <u>13 lbs.</u> |
| | 75 lbs. |

This may seem like a lot of powdered milk, but note that the milk will be used primarily as an ingredient in making meals.

Cooking with the Basics

Okay. So you have begun stocking the basics. What's the next step? Learning to cook with the basics. Even here, what you can make will be limited. You can make many of the breads found in chapter 3. You can also make many breakfast foods, cream of wheat cereal, oatmeal.

## BREAKFAST

### Wheat Cereal

Soak wheat overnight in cold water. For each cup of wheat berries, use one quart of water. Cook until soft. Serve with reconstituted milk and honey.

### Oatmeal

Soak oatmeal overnight in cold water. For each cup of oatmeal, use one quart of water. Add salt. Cook for 30 minutes. Serve with milk and honey.

### Cornmeal Porridge

Simmer corn meal in reconstituted milk. For each cup of cornmeal, use one quart of milk. Add salt. Stir constantly to avoid lumps. Serve with brown sugar.

## LUNCH

### Cream of Pea Soup

Cook 1 cup of peas in 1 quart of water. Add 1 Tbs. milk powder and 1 Tbs. flour. Gently simmer, stirring constantly. Serve with freshly baked whole wheat bread. (See recipe in Chapter 3.)

# DINNER

**Beans and Rice**

Soak beans overnight. Cook until tender. Prepare rice. (Add two cups water for every cup of rice, along with a dash of salt. Simmer for 20 minutes or until rice is tender.) Serve with freshly baked cornbread.

Now this menu may not appear terribly limited at first. But there are three things conspicuously missing:

1. Spices
2. Fruits and Veggies
3. Meat

Breakfast, regardless of whether you are making oatmeal or cream of wheat, is better with fruit. Soup is better with spices and veggies. And certainly beans and rice taste better when well seasoned with some spices and some meat.

Question: Do you think your family would be content without fruits, veggies and meats? If you are reading this book, then you have already answered this question for yourself. You don't want your family to just survive. You want your family to flourish. You want your family to sit down and enjoy a meal together. Whatever stressors life brings post-collapse, food need not be one of them. With some forethought and careful planning, you can ensure that your family thrives.

## CHAPTER 2: BREADS

**Sourdough Starter (Judy, Another One)**

Ingredients:

2 cups lukewarm milk (or non-chlorinated water)

2 cups flour

2 ½ tsp. yeast (one envelope)

Directions:

If you are not dairy-challenged and want starter that tastes more sour, use milk. Whisk everything together in glass or plastic bowl with a tight fitting lid. I used a half-gallon pickle jar. Place in a warm draft free place and stir once a day for 4 to 7 days. The mixture will bubble and can overflow the container so setting it on a plate or in a pan is advisable. If your starter ever changes to a purple color throw it out and start over!

After 4 to 7 days (7 is better) remove at least 1 cup and feed the starter. For every cup of starter removed replace it with 1 cup water or milk and 1 cup flour. It was recommend to alternate milk and water as you were feeding the starter. As I am dairy-challenged, all I used was water and the starter was just fine. Let your starter set for one day after feeding and refrigerate. Feed your starter at least once a week. If you can't use it once a week or are going to be gone freeze it. When you are ready to use it again thaw it in the refrigerator and then remove a cup and feed it. It will take several cycles to develop a true sourdough flavor. One of the recommendations I read while researching making sourdough starters years ago that made sense to me was; when starting and feeding use the same flours I would use while baking breads. So I used a 50/50 blend of whole wheat and bread flour with great results.

You can also mix the flour and potato water and set it on a counter and stir it every day to capture wild yeast in the air. Sometimes you have good results and sometimes not so good.

# Cornbread (Gayle)

*Yield: one loaf*

Ingredients:

| | |
|---|---|
| 1¼ cup flour | ¼ cup oil |
| ¾ cup corn meal | 2 egg whites |
| ½ cup sugar | 2 tsp. baking powder |
| dash of salt | 1 cup milk |

Directions:

Combine dry ingredients and mix well. Stir in reconstituted milk, eggs and oil. Pour batter in greased 5 x9 pan and cook for 35 minutes at 400 degrees.

# Crackers (Repair Momma)

*Yield: 20 crackers*

Ingredients:

      1 cup water

      4 Tbs. oil

      2 2/3 Tbs. sugar

      1 tsp. salt

      2 1/3 cups whole wheat flour

Directions:

Mix together water, oil, sugar, and salt. Add flour. Stir well and roll out dough to 1/4-inch thickness. Cut into 2-inch squares and poke several holes in each square with a fork. Bake 35 minutes at 350 degrees.

# Whole Wheat Biscuits (Gayle)

*Yield: one dozen*

Ingredients:

| | |
|---|---|
| 1 cup all purpose flour | 2 Tbs. sugar |
| 1 cup whole wheat flour | dash of salt |
| 4 tsp. baking powder | 1 cup milk |
| 2 Tbs. butter powder | |

Directions:

Combine dry ingredients and mix well. Stir in milk until moistened. Turn out onto a lightly floured surface and knead for 2 minutes. Roll to a thickness of ¾ inch and cut with a biscuit cutter. Place on ungreased cookie sheet and bake for 15-20 minutes at 350 degrees.

## Sourdough Biscuit (Judy, Another One)

Ingredients:

2 cups sourdough starter

1/4 cup oil

2 cups all purpose flour

1 Tbs. baking powder (optional)

3 Tbs. sugar

1 tsp. salt

Directions:

Mix wet ingredients together. In separate bowl whisk dry ingredients together. Add dry ingredients to wet and stir. Knead on a floured surface adding water or flour until dough ball is not sticky feeling. Let dough rest 10 minutes, then pinch off and form golf ball sized dough balls. Place in a well grease 12 inch dutch oven (9 x 13 pan) , cover, and let rise 1/2 hour. If not using baking powder knead 10 minutes and the rising time is 1 hour or until biscuits are double. Bury dutch oven in coals bake 15 to 25 minutes checking every now and then until golden brown on top. Or bake at 375 degrees for 30 to 35 minutes or golden brown.

# Homemade Rolls (Repair Momma)

*Yield: 16 rolls*

Ingredients:

 1/2 cup shortening

 1/2 cup sugar

 1 tsp. salt

 2 pkg. yeast

 5 cup flour, divided

 2 eggs

Directions:

Combine first shortening, sugar, salt, yeast and 2 cups flour in a large bowl; cut with pastry cutter. Beat eggs in a 2-cup measuring cup and fill cup with hot water up to the 2-cup mark. Pour over dry mixture. Slowly add remaining three cups flour. Cover. Let Rise 20 min. in warm oven. Pour onto floured surface. Knead. Flatten with hands into large pizza shape. Cut with pizza cutter into16 slices. Roll up from wide end to point. Place in greased pans leaving space for rolls to double in size. (You can shape like crescent or lay on side where swirl shows.) Cover. Let rise in warm oven at least 20 min. Remove from oven. Preheat oven. Preheat oven to 375. Bake 20-30 min. depending on how dark you prefer. Immediately brush with 1 stick (1/2 c.) melted butter.

# Wheat Sourdough Bread (Judy, Another One)

*Yield: 2 loaves*

Ingredients:

3/4 cup cracked wheat (or old fashion oats)

1 cup hot water

1/4 cup butter, melted (or vegetable oil)

2 Tbs. molasses

2 Tbs. honey

3/4 cup nonfat milk

1 1/2 tsp. salt

2 Tbs. ground flax seed

1/2 cup raw sunflower seeds (or pumpkin seeds)

2 1/2 cups sourdough starter

2 cups whole wheat flour

3 1/2 cups bread flour

1 egg, beaten with 1 Tbs. water (optional)

Directions:

In a medium bowl place cracked wheat or oats and pour hot water over and stir. Add melted butter or oil, molasses, honey, nonfat milk, and seeds and mix well. Cool to lukewarm and stir in sourdough starter. Stir in the flours one cup at a time starting with the whole wheat. When dough stiffens turn onto a floured surface and knead for 10 to 12 minutes working in as little of the flour as necessary. When the dough is smooth and elastic shape in a ball and place in a greased bowl, turning to grease all side. Cover and place in a draft free, warm spot to raise until double. Punch down and let rise again until double. When second rise is done punch down again and shape in to 2 loaves. Place into greased bread pans and let rise again until double or the dough reaches the tops of the pans. Brush tops with egg wash. Bake in a preheated oven at 375 degrees for 30 minutes. Cool 10 minutes in pans, then turn out to cool completely on racks.

# Whole Wheat Bread (UTmom)

*Yield: 4 loaves*

Ingredients:

| | |
|---|---|
| 6 cups very warm water | 1/3 cup gluten flour |
| 16 cups whole wheat flour | 2/3 cup canola oil |
| 2 Tbs. salt | 2/3 cup honey |
| 2 Tbs. dry active yeast | 2 Tbs. dough enhancer |

Directions:

Grind 10 cups of whole wheat into flour. I use some white wheat and some red wheat, but it doesn't matter. This will make approximately 16 cups of flour. Put 6 cups very warm water into your mixer. Add 6 cups freshly ground flour. Make sure dough hook is in place. Mix briefly then stop. Add 2 T. salt, 2 heaping T. dry active dry yeast, 1/3 cup gluten flour, 2/3 cup canola oil, 2/3 cup honey, and 2 T dough enhancer. While mixer is on low speed (I use speed 2 or 3 on my mixer) gradually add about 10 more cups wheat flour. Dough will slowly begin to pull away from sides of bowl. Allow mixer to knead the dough for approx. 10 minutes. With oil on hands, remove kneaded dough from mixing bowl. The dough should be elastic. Place on oiled surface, cut in to four even sections, form into loaves and place in pans. Note: One of the four sections may be used to make 6 dinner rolls.

Let rise in warm place until double in size. In the meantime, preheat your oven to 350 degrees. Bake for 30 minutes. Remove immediately from pans and place on cooling racks.

## Variation: Cinnamon Raisin Wheat Bread

I usually make one or two loaves out of each batch into cinnamon-raisin bread. After dividing the dough, roll one section out into a rectangle. Sprinkle with cinnamon so it covers the dough. Add some sugar and then raisins. Using the rolling pin, roll the raisins into the dough a little so that they stick. Roll up the dough into a loaf and place in pan. Bake like regular wheat bread.

# Oatmeal Bread (Gayle)

Ingredients:

    1 cup oatmeal

    1 cup whole wheat flour

    2 tsp. baking powder

    ½ tsp. salt

    1 Tbs. brown sugar

    2 Tbs. honey

    1 Tbs. oil

    1 cup liquid milk

Directions:

Grind oatmeal into flour. In a large bowl, combine oatmeal, flour, baking powder and salt. In a separate bowl, mix brown sugar, honey and oil. Then add reconstituted milk. Combine mixtures. Form a ball and cook on a greased cookie sheet for 20 minutes at 450 degrees

## Whole Wheat Tortillas (UTmom)

Ingredients:

      3 cups whole wheat flour

      1 Tbs. baking powder

      1/3 cup solid shortening

      1 tsp salt

      1 cup warm water
Directions:

Mix flour, baking powder, shortening and salt together in a bowl. Rub the mixture together with your fingers until it forms small crumbs. Add the warm water gradually and mix with a fork. Add some additional flour and knead by hand for a few minutes until the dough is smooth. Divide the dough into 12 balls, set them on a plate, cover with plastic wrap and let sit for 30 minutes.

On a lightly floured surface, roll each ball with rolling pin into a thin circle. Bake on a very hot, ungreased griddle until lightly freckled, about 30 seconds per side.

These can be a good substitute for bread. You can also sprinkle with coarse salt before cooking, cook them longer until they are crunchy and use as crackers.

# Indian Fry bread (TG)

Ingredients:

     1 cup flour

     1/4 tsp salt

     1 tsp powdered milk

     1 tsp baking powder

     1/2 cup water

     Oil for frying

Directions:

Sift dry ingredients together. Add water mixing well, but do NOT knead. Cut into 4 equal pieces and stretch into 5-7 inch disks. Heat oil to about 350 degrees. Fry dough pressing lightly to submerge, flip and fry the other side, usually 3 to 4 minutes.

# Whole Wheat Banana Bread with Glaze (Gayle)

*Yield: One loaf*

Ingredients:

> 3 Bananas, Mashed (or 1 ½ cup banana chips reconstituted and mashed)
>
> 1/3 cup butter
>
> 1 egg (2 Tbs. egg powder)
>
> 1 cup sugar
>
> 1 tsp vanilla
>
> 1 ½ cup flour
>
> 1 tsp. baking soda
>
> pinch of salt

Directions:

Mix bananas and butter. Add egg, sugar, and vanilla. Combine remaining ingredients and mix until flour is moistened. Do not over mix. Pour into greased 5 x 9 pan. Bake for one hour at 350 degrees.

## Glaze

Ingredients:

> 1 or 2 banana2, mashed (or ½ cup banana slices reconstituted and mashed)
>
> ¾ cup butter
>
> 3 cups confectioner's sugar
>
> 1 ½ tsp. vanilla

Directions:

Wisk mixture. Add a teaspoon of water if necessary to get proper consistency. Pour over cooled cake.

# Blueberry Muffins (Gayle)

*Yield: 1 Dozen*

Ingredients

| | |
|---|---|
| ¾ cup milk | 1 cup all purpose flour |
| ¼ cup oil | 1 cup whole wheat flour |
| ¼ cup honey | 3 tsp. baking soda |
| 2 Tbs. egg powder | dash of salt |
| 1 cup reconstituted blueberries | |

Directions

Mix milk, oil and honey. Add flour, soda, salt and egg powder. Mix until dry ingredients are moistened. Do not over mix. Fold in blueberries. Pour into greased muffin pan and bake 20 minutes at 400 degrees.

## Pumpkin Cranberry Bread (TG)

Ingredients:

3 cups flour

1 Tbs & 2 tsp. pumpkin pie spice

2 Tbs. baking soda

1 1/2 tsp. salt

1 can (15 oz) pumpkin

1 cp vegetable oil

3 cps sugar

4 large eggs

1/2 cp orange juice or water

1 can jellied cranberry sauce

Directions:

In one bowl combine flour, pumpkin pie spice, baking soda, and salt. In another bowl combine sugar, pumpkin, eggs, oil and juice (or water), beat just until blended. Add pumpkin mix to flour mix, stir just until moistened. Fold in cranberries. Spoon batter into a greased and floured 5 x 3 pan. Bake for 50-55 minutes. Cool for 10 minutes in pan then transfer to wire rack. (This is very important; if you don't cool it in the pan first it will stick). Also do not pour batter into the pan until it is ready to go into the oven. One year we made up a bunch at once and had it sitting in the pans waiting to go into the oven, it stuck so bad that I had to completely re-do it.

# Quick Beer Bread (Mark)

Ingredients:

       3 cups flour

       4 1/2 tsp. baking powder

       1 1/2 tsp. salt

       3 Tbs. sugar

       1 can 12 oz beer, room temperature

       4 Tbs. of butter for topping (optional)

Directions:

Combine the flour, sugar, and beer in a small bowl. Do not overmix. Overmixed batter results in tough bread. Mix with a wooden spoon or spatula just enough to combine all of the ingredients – a few lumps are fine. Scrape it into a well-greased loaf pan. Bake at 375°F for 60 minutes. Pour the melted butter over the top and bake 10 minutes longer. Cool in the pan for 10 minutes, then remove to a wire rack. If the loaf cools completely in the pan, condensation will make it soggy.

# CHAPTER 3: SOUPS

## Magic Mix (Bitsy)

Magic Mix is a combo of powdered milk, flour and butter. Place in sealed container and place in frig.

Ingredients:

2 1/3 cup powdered milk

1 cup flour

1 cup chilled butter (or reconstituted butter powder)

Directions:

Combine in a large bowl. Mix until it looks like cornmeal. Store in airtight container in fridge.

# Magic Mix: Replaces Condensed Canned Soup (Kate from Ga.)

Ingredients:

1/3 cup powdered milk

1/4 cup flour

1 Tbs. chicken bullion

1 Tbs. dry onion flakes

1 Bay leaf

1 tsp Mrs. Dash seasoning

1 cup milk


For cream of mushroom soup, add 2 Tbs. freeze dried mushrooms.

For cream of broccoli soup, add 2 Tbs. freeze dried broccoli

For cream of chicken soup, add 1 Tbs. chicken gravy powder.

For tomato soup, add 1 Tbs. tomato powder.

# Potato Soup (Kate in Ga.)

Ingredients:

> 1/2 cup canned butter
>
> 3 Tbs. onion powder or minced onion
>
> 2 Tbs. Powdered garlic
>
> 5 chicken bullion cubes
>
> 10 1/2 cups water
>
> Instant potato flakes

Directions:

In a large saucepan, add water, bullion cubes, butter, onion and garlic. Bring to a boil. Slowly add potato flakes 1/2 cup at a time, stirring constantly until you reach desired consistency. (Sometimes I make a thinner soup and sometimes I make it really thick.) Garnish with shredded cheddar cheese, bacon bits and/or chives.

Minced onion makes a lumpy soup and onion powder makes a smooth soup.

# Lentil Stew (Vienna Soggy Prepper)

Ingredients:

 1 cup lentils

 1 cup whole wheat berries  (soaked overnight)

 1 can diced tomatoes (or 1 ½ cup tomato powder and 3 ½ cups water)

 1 pint canned hamburger

 ½ cup dehydrated onion

 2 tsp. garlic

 2 Tbs. brown sugar

 2 Tbs. chili powder

 1 tsp. Italian Seasoning

 1 Bay leaf

 Salt and pepper to taste

Directions:

Add ingredients to pot and cover with water. Simmer for an hour or so, adding water as necessary. Serve with fresh bread, butter and honey.

# Jambulaya (STL Grandma)

Ingredients:

1 pint canned smoked sausage (andouille sausage)

1 pint canned chicken

1 tbsp dried garlic

1/3 cup dried onion

1 1/2 cups rice

1/3 cup dried green pepper

1 quart canned whole tomatoes

1 quart chicken broth  (or 4 cups water and 2 bullion cubes)

1 tsp chili powder

1 tsp red pepper flakes

3 dashes of hot sauce

1 Tbs. Worchestershire sauce

1 small can tomato paste

Olive oil as needed

Directions:

Brown Chicken and Sausage together with one or two Tbs. olive oil in large spaghetti pot (with lid) while rehydrating all the dried foods.  Add rehydrated onions, garlic and peppers and scrap up all the browned bits from the bottom of the pot and cook until the onions are tender on low heat.  Add all of the rest of the ingredients and crush the tomatoes before adding.  Cook covered until rice is done and tender - usually 1/2 hour or so - stirring every so often to keep bottom from burning.  Serve with cornbread - feeds 4 hearty eaters.

# Pasta e Fragioli (Gayle)

Ingredients:

| | |
|---|---|
| 1 cup red beans | 1 Tbs cup dehydrated onion |
| 1 cup white beans | 1 Tbs dehydrated carrots |
| 1 pint canned ground beef | 1 Tbs dehydrated celery |
| 1 quart spaghetti sauce | dash of oregano |
| 1 pint tomatoes | dash of garlic |
| 4 cups beef broth | 1 ½ cup elbow macaroni |

Directions:

Soak beans overnight, rinse and drain. Cook until almost tender. Add remaining ingredients except macaroni. Add macaroni 20-30 minutes before serving.

# Lamb and Veggie Stew (Farmgal)

Ingredients:

2 quarts lamb or beef broth

2 lbs cubed lamb stew meat

2 quarts tomato sauce

1 pint diced tomato

2 large onions

10-12 medium potatoes, peeled and diced

5-6 diced carrots

1 large yellow-fleshed rutabaga

5-6 celery stocks

3 Tbs. oil

3-4 gloves of garlic, peeled and diced

Handful of dried mushrooms (or small box of fresh mushrooms, sliced)

Dollop of horseradish

Dash of salt and pepper

Directions:

Heat the oil, brown the meat, cook the onion till clear, then added 2 quarts of homemade basic tomato sauce, or 2 cans of V8 will also work, plus 2 quarts of lamb or beef broth.

Spices -Salt, Pepper, Basil, and for me, Horseradish and Stinging Nettle Dried Leaves crumbled with a dash of hot mustard powder. If it still seems a little light in color or lacking depth to the broth, add a spoon of instant coffee to it.

Simmer for at least 40 min, and then pressure can, if you are going to eat it, ideally should simmer at least two hours or more and goes really well with dumplings on top. Its done when the meat is fork tender.

# Black Bean Soup (Daisy)

Ingredients:

      1 cup of dried black beans

      1 large can of diced tomatoes

      2 Tbs. of chili powder

      1 can of corn

      1/4 cup of dehydrated bell pepper

      1/4 cup dehydrated onion

      Salt and garlic powder to taste

      6 cups of water

Directions:

Mix all ingredients except corn into a large pot. Bring to a boil and then simmer, with a lid on, for about 4-6 hours. Add corn during the last hour so it stays firm. We eat this with corn bread or corn tortillas.

# Chicken Tortilla Soup (Kansas Proud)

Ingredients:

    1 quart chicken

    1 Tbs. garlic

    2 Tbs. dehydrated onion

    1 quart tomatoes

    1 Tbs. ground cumin

    1 Tbs. chili powder

    6 cups chicken broth

    1 tsp. salt

    1/2 tsp. oregano

    1/2 tsp rosemary

Directions:

In a large stock pot combine chicken, chicken stock, tomatoes, garlic and onion. Bring to a boil. Reduce heat and simmer 30 minutes. Add seasoning. Simmer 20 minutes. Serve with tortilla chips.

# Ham and Bean Soup (Bitsy)

Ingredients:

1 cup dry white beans (or two cans white beans)

1/3 cup dehydrated onion

1/3 cup dehydrated carrot

2 Tbs. olive oil

1 cup water

1 cup chicken broth

1 1/2 cups cubed ham (like Dak)

Salt and pepper to taste

Bay leaf

Ham bullion

Directions:

Note: Use either Great Northern Beans or Navy Beans. If using dry beans, soak beans overnight, rinse and cook. Mash half the beans. In soup pot, combine all ingredients. Cook over medium heat until vegetables soft. (I like to simmer extra long to let flavors meld.) Discard bay leaf before serving.

# Split Pea Soup (Gayle)

Ingredients:

     1 can ham

     1 cup split peas

     2 onion (or 2 Tbs. dehydrated onion)

     2 tsp. oil

     1 tsp. marjoram

     Salt and pepper to taste

Directions:

In a soup pan sauté onions in oil and then add split peas and diced ham. Cover with water. Add spices. For heartier soup, add dehydrated carrots, celery and potato.

# Mixed Bean Soup (Gayle)

Ingredients:

| | |
|---|---|
| 3 cups dry beans | 1 Tbs. garlic |
| 3 quarts chicken broth | 2 tsp. onion powder |
| 1 ½ cup onion (1 ½ Tbs. dehydrated) | 2 tsp. adobo sin pimienta |
| 2 cups carrots (2 Tbs. dehydrated) | 1 tsp. season pepper |
| 1 cup celery (1 Tbs. dehydrated) | 1 cups rice |
| 1 canned ham, diced | 1 cup lentils |

Directions:

Soak beans overnight, rinse and drain. Put beans in crock pot with chicken broth and all remaining ingredients except rice. Cook until beans are almost tender. About 30 minutes before dinner, add rice and lentils. Cook until rice is tender.

If pressure canning, omit rice and lentils.

# Chili (Gayle)

Ingredients:

       1 ½ cup small red beans

       2 lbs. hamburger

       1 lb. andouille sausage

       2 onion (or 3 Tbs. dehydrated)

       1 green pepper (or 2 Tbs. dehydrated)

       3 Stocks celery (or 1 Tbs. dehydrated)

       1 ½ tsp. cumin

       1 ½ chili powder

       1 Tbs. garlic

       1 tsp. onion powder

       1 ½ tsp. paprika

Directions:

If using fresh ground beef, brown beef and add andouille sausage. Add veggies and cook until tender. Add spices. Let cook 30 minutes. Serve with cornbread. To make this dish go further, serve on rice.

# Chicken Soup (Gayle)

Ingredients:

| | |
|---|---|
| 5 lbs. bone in chicken | 1 Tbs. garlic |
| 2 cups onion | 2 tsp. onion powder |
| 1 cup celery | 2 tsp. adobo sin pimienta |
| 1 cup carrots | 1 tsp. season salt |
| 1 pint andouille sausage | 1 tsp. season pepper |
| 1 pint kielbasa | 1 cup rice (or 3 cups egg noodles) |

Directions:

Boil chicken for 20 minutes in large stock pot. Remove chicken pieces and reserve chicken stock. (If you have time, allow chicken stock to cool. Then place in frig overnight. Skim off fat in the morning. Return to room temperature.) Debone chicken. Return to chicken stock. Add remaining ingredients and cook on low for several hours. Add noodles or rice 30 minutes before dinner.

Variation: Add whatever soup vegetables you have on hand—potatoes, yellow squash, zucchini, mushrooms, green beans, lima beans, turnip, etc.

If pressure canning, omit rice and noodles.

# Hearty Egg Drop Soup (AZ Rookie Prepper)

Ingredients:

½ dehydrated corn

4 eggs (4 Tbs. egg powder)

2 cups chicken broth

2 tsp. soy sauce

2 tsp. corn starch

A couple chives

A couple green onion

Salt and pepper to taste

Directions:

Rehydrate 1/2 cup of dehydrated corn. Mix up enough dehydrated egg for the equivalent of 4 regular eggs (4 Tbs. egg powder).

In a separate pot, boil enough water for 2 cups of broth made from chicken bullion. Add 2 teaspoons soy sauce. Slowly pour liquid egg mixture into the boiling broth. Add 2 teaspoons of corn starch to 2 to 3 tablespoons water and stir until cornstarch is dissolved, add that to boiling soup mixture. Put in rehydrated corn. Turn off heat. For a heartier dish, add canned chicken. Season with black pepper, chives or dried green onion, and salt to taste.

# Russian Soldier Soup (Ron)

Ingredients:

Sauerkraut with liquid

Carrots Chunks

Potato Chunks

Beef Chunks

Onions Chunks

Garlic Powder

Salt and pepper to taste

Polish Sausage (optional)

Directions

Add ingredients to large soup pot. Cover with water. Simmer until vegetables are soft. Serve with freshly baked bread.

# Apple Pumpkin Soup (TG)

Ingredients:

2 cps finely chopped tart apple

1/2 cp finely chopped onion

2 Tbs. butter

1 Tbs. flour

4 cups chicken broth

3 cups canned pumpkin

1/4 cup brown sugar packed

1/2 tsp each cinnamon, nutmeg, and ginger

1 cup unsweetened apple juice

1/2 cup half and half (can substitute evaporated milk)

1/4 tsp each salt and pepper

Directions:

In large sauce pan, sauté apples and onion in butter until tender, stir in flour until blended. Gradually whisk in chicken broth. Stir in pumpkin, brown sugar, and spices. Bring to a boil. Reduce heat, cover and simmer for about 25 minutes. Allow to cool slightly

# CHAPTER 4: CANNING

## Introduction

There are a number of excellent books and websites on canning. (There is a list of recommended books at the end of this chapter.) This chapter is not intended to cover the topic of canning in a comprehensive fashion. Rather this chapter aims to provide an introduction to canning and to highlight the significance of putting up food as an essential prep.

There are two types of canning: water bath canning and pressure canning. Water bath canning is used to can high acid foods such as pickles, salsas, chutneys and jellies. Pressure canning is used to can low acid foods, meats and soups. In this chapter, we will consider each method in turn.

## Water Bath Canning

To begin canning utilizing the water bath method, all that is needed is a large stockpot, some canning jars and canning utensils. If you wish, you may purchase a water bath canner. This has the advantage of having a wire rack on which filled jars sit during the canning process. (If you use a large stockpot as a water bath canner, you will need some contraption that sits in the bottom of the pot that the jars rest on—I used a metal steamer.)

One important point, when utilizing either the water bath method or the pressure canning method is to follow the recipe precisely. Never reduce the amount of salt, sugar or vinegar in a recipe. The amount specified in the recipe is necessary to prevent the growth of bacteria. It is also important to use pickling salt. Do not use table salt, as table salt contains additives that may turn the liquid cloudy.

With water bath canning, it is important to sterilize the jars. Only use proper canning jars. You may reuse the jars and the screw ring, but you will need to purchase new lids each time you use a jar. To sterilize jars, fill stockpot or water bath canner with water. Place room temperature jars in lukewarm water. Turn on heat and bring to a rapid boil. Jars are sterilized after 10 minutes of rapid boil. Place the screw rings and the lids in a separate pot, and sterilize by simmering for five minutes. Use proper canning utensils when removing hot jars and lids from pots.

After filling jars, remember to wipe the rim of the jar with a clean paper towel, as food particles can prevent the lid from properly sealing. Remember to remove air bubbles before sealing jars. Place lid on jar, screw on screw ring and process in water bath for the recommended amount of time. When removing jars, use a proper jar lifter utensil. Place hot jars on protected surface (a towel on the kitchen counter) and leave to cool. The following morning, check seal by unscrewing screw ring and picking up jar by lid.

In this part of the chapter, we consider some popular foods that can be made with water bath canning including pickles, salsa, jam, chutney and pie filling. Specific recipes include bread & butter pickles, salsa, strawberry jam, peach jam, mango chutney, apple pie filling and cherry pie filling.

# Bread & Butter Pickles (Gayle)

*Yield: 9 pints*

Ingredients:

      6 lbs. small pickling cucumbers

      6 small onions, thinly sliced

      1 sweet green pepper, thinly sliced

      1 sweet red peppers, thinly sliced

      3 Tbs. pickling salt

      6 cups cider vinegar

      6 cups white sugar

      3 Tbs. whole mustard seeds

      1½ celery seeds

      ¾ tsp. turmeric

      ½ tsp. ground cloves

Directions

Prepare cucumbers by removing a thin slice from each end. Slice cucumbers, onions and peppers into thin slices (about 4 mm in thickness). Put down a layer of cucumbers, onions and peppers and sprinkle with salt. Do another layer, and sprinkle with salt. Then another layer, and sprinkle with salt. (The salt serves to draw the excess water out from the vegetables.) Let vegetables sit for three hours. Rinse twice and drain thoroughly.

In a stainless steel pan, add vinegar, sugar, mustard seeds, celery seeds, turmeric and cloves. Bring to a boil. Add vegetables and boil for 1 minute or until cucumbers become a dull green.

Remove sterilized jars from the canner and fill immediately. Pour liquid over vegetables leaving a ½ head space. Remove air bubbles. Process pint jars for 10 minutes and quart jars for 15 minutes.

# Chunky Garden Salsa (Gayle)

*Yield: 9 pints*

Ingredients:

> 6 lbs. peeled tomatoes, chopped
>
> 3 cups onions
>
> 10 cloves garlic, diced
>
> 1 ½ cups sweet red pepper, diced
>
> 2 Habenero or Scotch Bonnet peppers, diced
>
> 1 ½ cup red wine vinegar
>
> ¾ cup cilantro
>
> ½ cup orange juice
>
> ¼ cup lime juice
>
> 1 Tbs. white sugar
>
> 1 Tbs. pickling salt
>
> ¾ cup tomato paste

Directions:

Combine all ingredients except tomato paste in stainless steel pot. Bring to a gentle boil and cook uncovered for 30 minutes, stirring occasionally. Then stir in tomato paste and cook for an additional two minutes.

Remove sterilized jars from the canner and fill immediately, leaving ½ inch headspace. Remove air bubbles. Process pint jars for 20.

Note: When dicing hot peppers, wear surgical gloves and do not touch your face.

# Tomatillo Sauce, Verde (Judy, Another One)

Yield: 6 pints

Ingredients:

   6 cups tomatillos

   3 cups onion

   3 jalapeno peppers

   8 garlic cloves

   1/4 cup cilantro, chopped

   1/2 cup lime juice, lemon will work in a pinch

   1 tsp cumin, ground

   1 Tbsp salt

Directions:

Grind vegetables in a meat grinder on coarse or in a food processor. Combine all the ingredients in a large pot. Stir frequently over high heat until mixture comes to a boil. Reduce heat and simmer 20 minutes stirring occasionally. Ladle into pint jars. Leave 1/2 inch head space. Clean lip of jars and adjust lids process in a hot water bath for 20 minutes.

Note: If less heat is desired seed and remove veins of jalapenos; if more heat is desired, add more jalapenos. As always, wear rubber gloves when handling hot peppers. Cumin can be reduced to also cut the heat.

# Strawberry Jam (Gayle)

*Yield: 9 pints*

Ingredients:

       4 quarts strawberries, hulled

       4 tsp. grated lemon peel

       2 tsp. lemon juice

       2 pkg. powdered pectin

       14 cups white sugar

Directions:

In a bowl, crush enough strawberries to make 9 cups. Combine crushed strawberries, lemon peel, lemon juice and pectin in a large stainless steel pan. Bring to a boil, stirring frequently. Add sugar and return to a boil. Boil for one minute, stirring constantly.

Remove sterilized jars from canner and fill immediately, leaving ¼ inch headspace. Remove air bubbles. Process pint jars for 20 minutes.

# Peach Jam (Gayle)

*Yield: 9 pints*

Ingredients:

   4 quarts peaches, pealed

   1 cup water

   12 cup white sugar

Directions:

In a bowl, mash peaches and mix in water. Pour mixture into stainless steel pan and cook for 10 minutes. Add sugar and return to a boil. Boil for one minute, stirring constantly.

Remove sterilized jars from canner and fill immediately, leaving ¼ inch headspace. Remove bubbles. Process pint jars for 25 minutes.

# Mango Chutney (Gayle)

*Yield: 9 pints*

Ingredients:

      6 large apples, peeled, cored and chopped

      5 large mangos, peeled and chopped

      1 cup sweet red pepper, chopped

      3 cup white sugar

      2 cup onion

      1 cup golden raisins

      1¼ cup white vinegar

      ½ cup gingerroot, peeled and diced

      2 Tbs. lemon juice

      2 tsp. curry powder

      ½ tsp. salt

      ½ tsp. ground nutmeg

      ½ tsp. cinnamon

Directions:

Combine apples, mango, pepper, sugar, onion, raisins, vinegar and gingerroot in stainless steel pan. Bring to a gentle boil and cook uncovered for 20 minutes, stirring occasionally. Add lemon juice and spices. Boil for another five minutes.

Remove sterilized jars from canner and fill immediately, leaving ½ inch headspace. Remove bubbles. Process pint jars for 15 minutes.

## Apple Pie Filling (Gayle)

*Yield: 7 Quarts*

Ingredients:

  4 quarts water

  6 cups white sugar

  3 Tbs. ground nutmeg

  ½ cup cinnamon

  20 apples, peeled, cored and sliced

Directions:

Combine water and sugar in stainless steel pan and boil until sugar dissolves. Boil for five minutes. Add spices and sliced apples. Boil for an additional five minutes.

Remove sterilized jars from canner and fill immediately, leaving ½ inch headspace. Remove bubbles. Process quart jars for 30 minutes.

# Cherry Pie Filling (Gayle)

*Yield: 7 Quarts*

Ingredients:

      4 quarts water

      8 cups white sugar

      ¼ cup cornstarch

      1 cup water

      6 quarts cherries, cleaned and pitted

Directions:

Combine water and sugar in stainless steel pot and boil until sugar dissolves. Dissolve cornstarch in one cup of water, and slowly add to pot. Bring mixture to a gentle boil, stirring constantly until mixture thickens. Add cherries and boil for another five minutes.

Remove sterilized jars from canner and fill immediately, leaving ½ inch headspace. Remove bubbles. Process quart jars for 30 minutes.

# Pressure Canning

We now turn to pressure canning. The only safe way to process low acid foods such as tomatoes, meats and soups is with a pressure caner. The aim of this chapter is to provide motivation for learning to pressure can, to dispel some of the irrational fears surrounding pressure canning, to provide an overview of the process, and to list a few examples of pressure canning recipes.

I recommend that you read the owners manual that comes with your pressure canner before attempting to pressure can. I highly recommend *The Ball Blue Book: Guide to Preserving*. If you follow the instructions that come with your canner and read through the Ball book, and follow the instructions and recipes carefully, you will not have any problems.

*Why Learn to Pressure Can?*

Pressure canning is an important skill to learn, for without electricity the food in your freezer can last no more than a few days. If you have a pressure caner (and a means to cook), you can pressure can that meat. The result is shelf stable meats.

A pressure caner also gives you more options for stocking shelf stable meats. Without a pressure caner, you must either purchase tinned meats from the store or you must purchase freeze-dried meats, and that's not economically feasible for most people. In addition, if your local store has an incredible sale on meats but you do not have a lot of freezer space, you have the option of canning some or most of the meat.

In contrast to water bath canning, it is not necessary to sterilize the canning jars—just make sure the jars are clean. (Reference: All American Pressure Caner instruction manual, p. 40.) It is necessary to simmer the lids for five minutes, primarily to warm up the seal ring.

*Irrational Fears*

I can write about irrational fears surrounding pressure caning from personal experience. I put off purchasing a pressure caner out of fear that it would blow up my kitchen. But I did the research before buying, and I opted for the All American Pressure Caner primarily because the lid is affixed to the canner with wing nuts and there is a pressure blowout valve on the lid of the canner. So it's incredibly unlikely that the caner would blow up my kitchen.

I can tell you from experience that once you can your first batch using a pressure caner, you will laugh at yourself for being afraid. Just read the instructions carefully and follow a reputable recipe, and you will be fine.

*Overview of the Process*

Suppose you have made a large batch of chili and you want to can it. What do you do? Well, quite simply you just fill clean jars with chili, leaving a one-inch headspace. Then wipe the rim of the jar with a clean paper towel and put on lid and screw ring. Fill canner with recommended amount of water (typically 1 ½ to 2 inches). Put filled jars in canner. Affix lid and turn on burner. Allow the caner to get up to temperature and start the timer.

If you are using a weight gauge canner such as the All American, vent steam for the recommended amount of time (usually 10 minutes) and insert the proper weight depending on your altitude. (See instruction manual for details.) With the All American, you know the caner has reached the proper temperature when the pressure gauge rocks two or three times per minute.

That's it. When the timer goes off, turn off the burner and allow the caner to reduce to zero pressure naturally. Remove weight gauge. And then open caner. Use proper caning utensils to remove hot jars from caner. Place hot jars on a towel and allow to cool overnight. Test the seal in the morning. Label and put away.

Let us look at a couple of recipes for pressure canning

## Skinless Boneless Chicken Breast

*Yield: 10 pints*

Ingredients:

      10 lbs. raw chicken, cut in chunks

      1 tsp. salt

Directions:

Cut raw chicken into chunks. Pack into clean pint jars, leaving a one-inch headspace. Add 1 tsp. salt. Clean rim, and add lid and screw ring. Process at 10 lbs. of pressure in pressure caner for 75 minutes for pint jars and 90 minutes for quarts jars. Do not add liquid to caning jars; chicken will make its own liquid as it cooks. (If canning at an altitude above 1000, process at 15 pounds. Check instruction manual for details.)

## Skinless Boneless Chicken Breast and Andouille Sausage

*Yield: 10 Pints*

Ingredients:

> 8 lbs. raw chicken, cut in chunks

> 2 lbs. raw andouille sausage, diced

Directions:

Cut raw chicken into chunks. Dice sausage. Pack into clean pint jars, leaving a one-inch headspace. Add 1 tsp. salt. Clean rim, and add lid and screw ring. Process at 10 lbs. of pressure in pressure caner for 75 minutes for pint jars and 90 minutes for quarts jars. Do not add liquid to caning jars; chicken will make its own liquid as it cooks. (If canning at an altitude above 1000, process at 15 pounds. Check instruction manual for details.)

# Hamburger in Broth

*Yield: 10 pints*

Ingredients:

       10 lbs. hamburger

       5 cups water

       5 cubes beef bullion

Directions:

Prepare beef bullion. Set aside. Brown hamburger and drain grease. Pack cooked hamburger into jars and fill jars with beef broth leaving a one-inch headspace. Clean rim, and add lid and screw ring. Process at 10 lbs. pounds of pressure in pressure caner for 75 minutes for pint jars and 90 minutes for quarts jars. (If canning at an altitude above 1000, process at 15 pounds. Check instruction manual for details.)

# Hamburger in Dry Onion Soup Mix

*Yield: 10 pints*

Ingredients:

       10 lbs. hamburger

       5 cups dry onion soup mix prepared

Directions:

Prepare soup mix by adding boiling water. Set aside. Brown hamburger and drain grease. Pack cooked hamburger into jars and fill jars with soup leaving a one-inch headspace. Clean rim, and add lid and screw ring. Process at 10 lbs. pounds of pressure in pressure caner for 75 minutes for pint jars and 90 minutes for quarts jars. (If canning at an altitude above 1000, process at 15 pounds. Check instruction manual for details.)

# Hamburger and Andouille Sausage

*Yield: 10 pints*

Ingredients:

      8 lbs. hamburger

      2 lbs. andouille sausage

      5 cups beef broth

Directions:

Prepare beef bullion. Set aside. Brown hamburger and drain grease. Add sausage and cook for five minutes. Pack sausage-hamburger mix into jars and fill jars with beef broth leaving a one-inch headspace. Clean rim, and add lid and screw ring. Process at 10 lbs. pounds of pressure in pressure caner for 75 minutes for pint jars and 90 minutes for quarts jars. (If canning at an altitude above 1000, process at 15 pounds. Check instruction manual for details.)

# Rabbit or Squirrel

*Yield: 10 pints*

Ingredients:

      10 lbs. rabbit or squirrel

      5 cups beef broth

Directions:

Prepare broth. Skin animal and wash in salt water. Dry meat with cloth. Cut into chunks and fry until browned but not entirely tender. Add meat to jars and fill with broth, leaving a one-inch headspace. Clean rim, and add lid and screw ring. Process at 10 lbs. pounds of pressure in pressure caner for 75 minutes for pint jars and 90 minutes for quarts jars. (If canning at an altitude above 1000, process at 15 pounds. Check instruction manual for details.)

# For Further Reading

*Books*

[1]     Ball Blue Book of Canning: Guide to Preserving

[2]     Judi Kingry and Lauren Devine, The Ball Complete Book of Home Preserving

[3]     Ellie Topp an Margaret Howard, The Complete Small-Batch Preserving

Websites

[1]     National Center for Home Food Preservation, Complete Guide to Home Canning,
        http://www.uga.edu/nchfp/publications/publications_usda.html

[2]     Ball Website
        http://www.freshpreserving.com/home.aspx

[3]     Purdue University, Complete Guide to Home Cannini
        http://www.extension.purdue.edu/usdacanning/

[4]     Virginia Cooperative Extension, Boiling Water Bath Canning
        http://pubs.ext.vt.edu/348/348-594/348-594.html

[5]     National Center for Home Food Preservation, Using a Pressure Canner
        http://www.uga.edu/nchfp/publications/uga/using_press_canners.html

# CHAPTER 5: BREAKFAST

# Oatmeal (Gayle)

Ingredients

       3 cups water

       ¼ teaspoon salt

       1 ½ cup oats

       1 Tbs. milk powder (optional)

       2 tsp. honey (optional)

Directions:

Put water and salt in saucepan and bring to a boil. Add oatmeal. Cook for five minutes over medium heat, stirring to remove lumps. Remove from heat, and add milk powder and honey.

Variations: There are as many variations of oatmeal as there are people eating oatmeal. Here are some ideas: raisin and brown sugar, peaches and cream, applesauce or dehydrated apples, peanut butter and jelly, etc.

# Wheat Berry Cereal (Gayle)

Ingredients:

1 cup whole wheat berries

½ tsp. salt

3 cups water

1 Tbs. honey (optional)

Directions:

Soak wheat berries over night in three cups of water and ½ tsp. salt. Do not drain and rinse. Bring mixture to a boil and simmer for 30 minutes. Add honey, if desired.

Variations: Add any fresh or dehydrated fruit.

# Cream of Wheat (Gayle)

Ingredients:

    1 cup wheat, coarsely milled

    5 ½ cups water, divided

    ½ tsp. salt

    1 Tbs. oil

    1/3 cup dry milk

    1/3 cup white sugar

Directions:

In a medium bowl, mix 1 cup of water, 1 cup coarsely milled wheat, salt and oil. Heat 4 ¼ cups water in a saucepot and bring to a boil. Add wheat mixture to boiling water, stirring constantly. Simmer for 15 minutes or so. Add dry milk powder and sugar before serving.

Variation: Add any fresh or dehydrated fruit. Jam or jelly works well too.

# Basic Granola (Repair Momma)

Ingredients:

2 ½ cups of sugar

1 ½ cups water

6 Tbs. oil

1 ½ tsp. salt

10 cups rolled oats (uncooked)

Directions:

In a pan combine the sugar, water, oil and salt.  Heat until sugar is dissolved, but do not boil.  Pour syrup over the oats and stir until well coated.  Add a little more rolled oats if the texture seems to moist.  Place in pans or sheets about ½- inch thick.  Bake at 425 degrees, 20-30 minutes, stirring occasionally.  Bake 15 minutes longer if you want it crunchier.  Makes 11 cups.  Store in an airtight container.

# Coconut Almond Granola (TG)

Ingredients:

      3 Tbs. oil

      3 Tbs. honey

      1/4 tsp. almond extract

      2 cups quick oats

      3 tbs. flaked coconut

      3 tbs. powdered milk

      3 tbs. sliced almonds

Directions:

Combine oil, honey and extract. Stir in oats, coconut, and milk. Bake at 350 degrees in an ungreased 1 1/2 quart baking dish for 15-20 minutes or until golden brown, stirring occasionally. Stir in almonds. Cool. Store in a covered container.

# Pancake Mix (Candy in Nebraska)

Ingredients

8 cups All-purpose flour

3/4 cup Sugar

1/2 cups milk powder

2 tsp. salt

2 Tbs. baking powder

Directions:

Mix all ingredients together and store in a one-gallon air tight container. When ready to make pancakes take 1 2/3 cup to 2 cups of mix and add water to reach desired consistency.

## Whole Wheat Pancakes (Kate in Ga.)

Ingredients

1 ½ cup whole wheat flour

1/3 cup sugar

2 Tbs. milk powder

1 tsp. salt

5 Tbs. oil

1 /1/2 cup water

Directions:

Mix dry ingredients together. Add water and oil whisking until blended. Cook on nonstick griddle or greased fry pan. Cook one side until bubbles on the surface just begin to pop. Then turn.

Variations: Add reconstituted apple pieces, blueberries, chocolate chips, etc.

# Sourdough Pancakes (Judy, Another One)

Ingredients:

2 cups sourdough starter at room temperature

2 Tbs. sugar (or honey)

1/4 cup oil

2 Tbs. egg powder (or 1 egg)

1/2 tsp salt

1 tsp. baking soda

1 Tbs. warm water

Directions:

In a cup, mix water and soda. In a large bowl mix everything else well. When ready to cook pancakes gently fold in the baking soda solution. It will cause a foaming and raising action. Let mixture foam and bubble for a minute or two. Cook on a lightly greased hot griddle using a 1/4 to a 1/2 cup of batter per pancake until golden brown on each side.

Variations: Before adding the baking soda mixture to the batter, add the following. Combine 1 cup blueberries with the 2 Tbs. of sugar let stand a few minutes and gently fold into batter. I've used cherries and raspberries from the garden with success. Chop an apple or two in the batter with a 1/2 tsp cinnamon. Slice or mash banana and 1/2 cup chopped nuts folded into the batter. Sprinkle chocolate chips on the batter when first poured on the griddle. Cook on one side until golden brown then turn and cook on other side.

## Whole Wheat Gingerbread Pancakes with Carmel Sauce (Kate in Ga.)

Ingredients:

2 cups whole wheat flour

4 Tbs. powdered eggs (or 2 whole eggs)

1 1/2 tsp baking soda

1/2 tsp salt

3 cups apple juice

1/4 cup vegetable oil

Directions:

Mix dry ingredients together. Add apple juice, whisking until blended. Add vegetable oil. Wisk again. Cook one side until bubbles on the surface just begin to pop. Then turn.

Variations: Add reconstituted apple pieces, blueberries, chocolate chips, etc.

## Carmel Sauce

Ingredients:

1/2 cup butter powder

1 1/2 cups sugar

2 Tbs. corn syrup

2 tsp. vanilla

3/4 cup buttermilk (use powdered – then reconstitute.)

Directions:

I also add a bit extra water to get the correct consistency. However, if you reconstitute the butter powder that won't be necessary. I never bother to reconstitute anything; I just use extra water if necessary.

Place all ingredients except vanilla in an extra large saucepan. (This will create a LOT of foam so be sure to use a big pan.) Bring to a boil and cook for 7 minutes. Stir constantly to prevent scorching. Remove from heat and add vanilla extract.

# Oatmeal Almond Pancakes (TG)

Ingredients:

1 1/4 cup flour

3/4 cup quick rolled oats

3 Tbs. sugar

1 1/2 cup evaporated milk

3 Tbs. oil

2 large eggs

1/2 tsp almond extract

1/2 tsp. cider or white wine vinegar

1/2 cup slivered almonds, roasted

Directions:

Mix all dry ingredients, except almonds. In a separate bowl mix all wet ingredients. Slowly incorporate dry into wet until moist, stir in almonds. Fry on griddle.

# American Toast (Gayle)

Ingredients:

    6 Tbs. whole egg powder

    1 cup milk, reconstituted

    2 tsp. white sugar

    ¼ tsp. salt

    6 slices bread

Directions:

Reconstitute egg powder in milk. Add  sugar and salt. Coat each side of bread with egg mixture and fry on griddle. Serve with maple or peach syrup.

Note: This is an excellent recipe to use leftover, day-old bread.

# Spam and Egg Wrap (Gayle)

Ingredients:

1 can spam, diced

¾ cup scrambled egg powder

1 cup water

2 Tbs. milk powder

1 Tbs. oil

Salt and pepper to taste

¾ cup freeze dried cheddar cheese (or canned cheese)

4 tortillas

Directions:

Warm oil in skillet, and fry up diced spam. In a separate bowl, reconstitute egg powder in 1 cup of water and mix in milk powder. Add egg mixture to browned spam. Add salt and pepper to taste. Cook on medium until eggs have set. Serve burrito style in homemade tortillas. (See Chapter 3 for tortilla recipe.)

# Breakfast Burritos (AZ Rookie Prepper)

Ingredients:

1 Tbs. real bacon bits (or dehydrated chicken or beef)

1 Tbs. oil

¾ cup scrambled egg powder

1 cup water

2 Tbs. milk powder

2 tsp. dehydrated bell pepper, reconstituted

2 tsp. dehydrated onion, reconstituted

Salt and pepper to taste

1 can beans (optional)

Salsa (optional)

4 tortillas

Directions:

Warm oil in skillet, and fry up bacon bits or other meat. In a separate bowl, reconstitute egg powder in 1 cup of water and mix in milk powder. Add reconstituted peppers and onions. Add egg mixture to browned meat. Add salt and pepper to taste. Cook on medium until eggs have set. Serve burrito style in homemade tortillas. (See Chapter 3 for tortilla recipe.)

## CHAPTER 6: DINNER

# Beef Stroganoff (Kate from Ga.)

Ingredients:

      1 lb. freezed dried or canned ground beef

      2 cups milk (use reconstituted powdered milk)

      1/3 cup cream cheese (or 1/3 cup sour cream powder)

      1 cup water

      2 cups elbow macaroni

      1/4 cups dried mushroom (optional)

      1/2 cup stroganoff mix (recipe below)

Directions:

Reconstitute the freeze dried beef, if necessary. Place meat in skillet and heat. When meat is ready, add the stroganoff mix, noodles, water and milk. Simmer 8 – 10 minutes covered. Stir once or twice during this time but always replace cover. When noodles are tender, add the cream cheese or reconstituted sour cream. Stir until smooth.

## Stroganoff mix

Ingredients:

| | |
|---|---|
| 1 cup powdered milk | 1 Tbs. garlic powder |
| 1 cup flour | 1Tbs parsley |
| 1/2 cup minced onions | 1 tsp thyme |
| 1 Tbs. onion powder | 1/2 tsp nutmeg |
| dash of salt | |

Directions:

This mix will make about seven dinners. Store in a vacuum-sealed canning jar.

# Shepherds Pie (Gayle)

Ingredients:

1 pint hamburger canned in beef broth

1 tsp. garlic

1 tsp. onion powder

1 tsp. paprika

1 tsp. season salt

½ tsp. season pepper

1 can carrots (or 2 Tbs. dehydrated carrots)

1 can corn (or 2 Tbs. dehydrated corn)

1 can peas (or 2 Tbs. dehydrated peas)

1 pkg. instant mashed potatoes

Directions:

In skillet, combine hamburger, carrots, corn and peas. Warm through. In a separate pan, prepare instant mashed potatoes. Fluff potatoes onto skillet mixture. Bake for 15 minutes at 400 degrees.

Variation: Replace hamburger with wheat. Boil 1 cup of wheat in 3 cups water, one bullion cube and ½ tsp. salt. Drain wheat. Add to stroganoff in place of hamburger.

# Smothered Chicken (Marebear)

Ingredients

3 to 4 chicken thighs or 2 leg quarters

1 can Mushroom soup

1 pkg. Lipton's Onion Soup Mix

3/4 cup of fresh orange juice

1/4 cup Harvey's Bristol Cream Sherry

3/4 cup of white rice, uncooked

Directions

Combine the mushroom soup, orange juice and sherry, whisking until smooth and blended. Add uncooked rice and mix. Pour into a 2 qt. casserole with a fitted glass lid. Remove skin & fat from chicken pieces. Sprinkle about 3/4 of the dry onion soup over rice mixture; add chicken pieces, and sprinkle remainder of onion soup. Bake covered for 75 minutes in 350° oven. Once done, remove chicken and stir the hot rice until blended before serving.

Makes two pig portions!

Cook's Notes: I like to use orange juice with heavy pulp such as Grovestand by Tropicana

# Asian Beef Noodles (Schatzie Ohio)

Ingredients:

    1 lb. canned beef tips

    1 jalapeno pepper, finely chopped

    1 Tbs. oil

    1 package (3 oz) beef flavor instant ramen noodles

    1/4 cup steak sauce (A1)

    1 Tbs. shredded carrot, reconstituted

    2 Tbs. chopped green onion, reconstituted

    1/4 cup chopped peanuts

Directions:

Cook noodles according to package directions and drain; reserve seasoning packet.
Combine jalapeno pepper, carrot, green onions in skillet and cook on medium heat. Add
steak sauce, seasoning packet and beef tips. Cook on medium until contents have
warmed. Do not overcook. Serve with peanuts sprinkled on top.

# Spam and Noodles (TG)

Ingredients:

1 Tbs. oil

1 can Spam

1 can corn or peas

2 packages Raman Noodles

Directions:

Prepare Raman Noodles according to package directions; drain and reserve seasoning packet. In a skillet, fry up diced Spam and veggie in 1 Tbs. oil and spice packet. Serve over Ramen noodles.

# Spaghetti with Meat Sauce (Gayle)

Ingredients:

   1 lb. freeze dried or canned hamburger

   1 quart spaghetti sauce

   1 pint tomatoes

   2 tbs. garlic powder

   1 tbs. onion powder

   ½ tbs. sugar

   1 pkg. spaghetti or vermicelli noodles

Directions:

Reconstitute the freeze dried beef, if necessary. Place meat in skillet and heat. When meat is ready, add spaghetti sauce and canned tomatoes. Heat through. Add garlic powder, onion powder and sugar. Serve over cooked noodles.

Variation: Replace hamburger with wheat. Boil 1 cup of wheat in 3 cups water, one bullion cube and ½ tsp. salt. Drain wheat. Add to stroganoff in place of hamburger.

## Putanessca Sauce over Linguini (Breadmomma)

Ingredients:

    1 cup sun dried tomatoes, julienated

    1/2 cup dried onion diced

    1 Tbs. dried sliced garlic

    1 cup red wine

    1 cup chicken stock

    1/2 cup tomato powder

    1/2 Tbs. cayenne pepper

    3 Tbs. capers

    3 Tbs. salt cured olives-pitted, sliced

    3 Tbs. olive oil

Directions:

Reconstitute onion and garlic in mixture of wine and stock. Sauté reconstituted vegetables in olive oil. Add olives, tomato powder and cayenne pepper. Simmer for 20 minutes. Add capers. Serve over linguini or other pasta.

# Chicken Penne (Jo (Georgia))

Ingredients:

1 Tbs. parsnips

2 Tbs. celery

1 Tbs. leeks

1 Tbs. ghee

1 ½ Tbs. mushrooms

1 pint chicken stock

4 cups water

1 Tbs. bacon fat

2 Tbs. flour

1 pint chicken

½ cup Parmesan cheese

1 pkg penne or other pasta

2Tbs. carrots

Salt and pepper

Directions:

Reconstitute parsnips, celery and leeks. In a skillet, prepare a blond roux. (Roux is a mixture of one part fat and two parts flour. In this case, the roux is made from a mixture of bacon fat and flour.) In a separate pan, simmer reconstituted veggies in ghee and then add chicken stock and water. Bring to a boil. Add Roux, stir in completely to eliminate lumps. Add mushrooms and pasta. About five minutes before pasta is done, add chicken and reconstituted carrots. Serve with grated Parmesan cheese.

# Cajun Red Beans and Rice (Gayle)

Ingredients:

2 Tbs. dehydrated celery

2 Tbs. dehydrated onion

2 Tbs. dehydrated green pepper

1 Tbs. canola oil

1 quart red beans

1 pint chicken and andouille sausage

1 Tbs. Cajun Spice Mix

1 cup rice

Directions:

Reconstitute celery, onion and pepper. Pour oil in skillet. Add veggies, beans, meat mixture and spice mixture. Simmer for 15 minutes. Mash contents. Serve over rice.

Meatless option: omit chicken and andouille sausage.

# Shrimp Etouffee (Gayle)

Ingredients:

1 cup canola oil

1 cup flour

1 ½ Tbs. dehydrated green pepper

1 ½ Tbs. dehydrated onion

1 ½ Tbs. dehydrated celery

1 cup chicken stock

5 cups water

1 can large shrimp

1 pint andouille sausage

1 pint chicken

2 Tbs. Cajun spice

2 cups of rice

Directions:

Reconstitute peppers, onion and celery. (This is known as the holy trinity in Cajun cooking.) Prepare roux. (Heat canola oil and slowly add flour. Cook roux stirring constantly until roux is a medium brown. This will take upwards of one hour.) Add reconstituted veggies and immediately begin adding water and chicken stock. Add water and chicken stock slowly. You want to form a nice gravy—not too think and not too runny. Add shrimp, sausage and chicken. Add Cajun spice. Serve over rice with freshly baked bread.

## Green Chile & Chicken Enchiladas (UTmom)

Ingredients:

1 Tbs. dried onion

½ cup water

½ can (4 oz) diced green chiles

1 can (14.5 oz) green chile enchilada sauce

2 cans (12-15 oz) chicken chunks, drained

12 whole wheat tortillas

Cheese Whiz, Velveeta or dried cheese sauce mix

1 can (28 oz) green chili enchilada sauce

1/2 cup dried cheese sauce mix

1 cup dried sour cream, reconstituted

Black olives

Directions:

Rehydrate onions in water for 15 min. then drain. Place in a large bowl with green chilis, green chili sauce (smaller can) and chicken chunks. Mix well. Spread each tortilla with cheese and 1/12 of the filling. Roll up burrito style.

Pour half of the 28 oz can of green chili sauce in bottom of 9x13 baking dish and place the rolled up tortillas on top in a single layer. Pour the remaining green chili sauce on top of the tortillas and sprinkle with ½ cup dried cheese sauce mix. Bake in preheated 350 degree oven for 30 minutes. Top each serving with sour cream, olives, etc.

# Beef, Rice & Bean, and Cheese Burrito (Judith)

Ingredients:

       1 lb. freezed dried or canned ground beef

       1 large onion (or 1 Tbs. dehydrated onion)

       Freeze dried or fresh cheese

       1 cup cooked rice

       1 cup refried beans

       Taco seasoning to taste

Directions:

Reconstitute the freeze dried beef, if necessary. Place meat and onion in skillet and heat. When meat is ready, add cooked rice and refried beans. Add taco seasoning. Serve on whole wheat tortilla. (See Chapter 3 for whole wheat tortilla recipe.)

## Bean Burrito Smothered in Chicken Chili Sauce (Gayle)

Ingredients:

1 pint chicken

2 Tbs. canola oil

1 can green chilies

1 tsp. chili powder

1 chicken bullion cube

1 can diced tomatoes

4 cups refried beans

8 flour tortillas

Directions:

In a skillet, heat oil and add flour to form a thick paste. Add chicken, green chilies, chili powder, tomatoes and chicken bullion. Cook five minutes over medium heat. Grease 9 x 13 baking pan. Put half a cup of refried beans in each tortilla and fold burrito style. Place burritos in baking pan. Cover with chili sauce. Bake for 30 minutes at 350 degrees.

# Black Bean Burrito (Gayle)

Ingredients:

2 tsp. oil

1 tsp. dehydrated onion, reconstituted

1 tsp. dehydrated green pepper, reconstituted

½ tsp. garlic powder

½ tsp. salt

1 can black beans

4 whole wheat tortillas

Directions:

Reconstitute onions and green peppers. Sauté in oil until lightly browned. Add beans and spices. Warm through and then mush beans. Serve on whole wheat tortilla. (See Chapter 3 for tortilla recipe.) Top with salsa, reconstituted sour cream and sprouts

# Black Beans and Rice

Ingredients:

       1 can black beans

       1 can corn

       1 pint tomato

       1 tsp. onion flakes

       ½ tsp. garlic powder

       1 cup rice

Directions:

In skillet, warm beans, corn, tomato and spices. Serve over cooked rice.

# Bean Burrito (Gayle)

Ingredients:

2 ½ cups dry pinto beans

3 quarts water

1 Tbs. dehydrated onion

2 Tbs. bacon fat

2 tbs. Cajun spice mix

Directions:

Soak beans overnight. Drain, rinse and cook in 3 quarts water until tender—usually about an hour. Add onions and bacon fat. With potato masher, mash beans. Add a little water if necessary for proper consistency. Add spice mix. Serve bean mix on flour tortilla. Top with salsa, reconstituted sour cream and bean sprouts.

## Macaroni and Cheese with Ham (Gayle)

Ingredients:

2 cup macaroni

½ cup cheese powder sauce

1 can evaporated milk

1 can ham

Directions:

Boil macaroni until just about tender. Drain and add cheese sauce and milk. Set aside. In a separate skillet, brown ham. Add browned ham to macaroni and cheese, and mix.

# Fried Rice (AZ Rookie Prepper)

Ingredients:

     1 cup canned meat (hamburger, chicken or ham)

     2 tsp. oil

     ¼ cup dehydrated peas

     ¼ cup dehydrated carrots

     1 Tbs. dehydrated onion

     ½ tsp. Chinese 5 Spice Seasoning

     Salt and pepper to taste

     1-2 tsp. soy sauce

     1 cup rice

Substitute for Chinese 5 Spice Seasoning

     2 tsp. of Szechuan ground peppercorns

     8 star anise, ground

     ½ tsp ground cloves

     1 Tbs. ground cinnamon

     1 Tbs. ground fennel seeds

Directions:

Prepare rice according to package directions. Sauté meat in skillet with oil. Add reconstituted veggies, rice, soy sauce and spices. If using any fresh veggies, add last, heat to readiness and enjoy.

# E-Z Chicken Casserole (Nuttbush)

Ingredients:

2 cans chicken

8 oz. sour cream (or equivalent amount of sour cream powder, reconstituted)

1 can cream of chicken soup (or Magic Mix with chicken bullion)

1 sleeve of Ritz crackers, crumbled

1/3 cup canned butter, melted

1 Tbs. dehydrated carrots

1 Tbs. dehydrated celery

1 Tbs. dehydrated onion

Directions:

Add some sliced onion, carrots and celery or approx. a TBS of each of the dehydrated vegetables and the chicken breasts to a pan of salted water and cook until breasts are cooked all the way through. Remove chicken from water (you can save the broth for another dish) and when cooled, cut up chicken into small pieces. (I actually shred my chicken into small pieces.) Place chicken in casserole dish and dump the cream of chicken soup and the sour cream into the dish and stir up the mixture. Make sure the sour cream and chicken soup have thoroughly blended. Smooth mixture evenly in the dish and pour the crumbled up Ritz crackers on top, completely covering the chicken mixture. Pour 1/3 cup melted butter over the cracker crumbles and if you like you can sprinkle poppy seeds on the top. Bake covered in a 350 degree oven for 30 minutes, removing the cover from the dish for the last five minutes.

**Cuban Rice and Chicken (Veee)**

Ingredients:

       1 cup cooked rice

       1 pint beans

       2 pints shredded chicken

       1 can Mexican corn, drained

       1 ½ tsp. Pulled Pork spice mix

Directions:

Cook rice. Add beans and shredded chicken and corn. Add spice mixture. (See chapter on spice mixes for Pulled Pork Spice recipe.)

## Santa Fe Bake (Kansas Proud)

Ingredients:

1 pint canned hamburger (optional)

1 quart canned tomato

1 pint salsa

1 can black beans, drained

1 can corn, drained

1 cup rice, cooked

Chopped black olives

Directions:

Prepare rice according to package directions. Mix all ingredients and bake at 350 degrees till done.

# Basic Rice, Beans, and Corn (Jim)

Ingredients:

　　1 cup rice

　　1 pint black beans (or ½ cup dried beans)

　　1 pint corn

　　1 tsp. cumin

　　2 tsp. fresh cilantro (optional)

　　1 tsp. lemon or lime juice (optional)

　　1 pint tomatoes (optional)

　　1 pint hamburger or chicken (optional)

Directions:

Cook one cup of rice. In a separate pan, mix beans and corn and then heat. Add cumin. Add optional ingredients, if using. Serve over rice.

# BBQ Beef Sandwich (UT mom)

Ingredients:

2 Tbs. dried onion

1 can beef chunks, (12-15 oz), liquid reserved

2 tsp. olive oil

½ cup ketchup

2 Tbs. brown sugar

¼ cup water

2 tsp. dried mustard

½ tsp. Worcestershire sauce

½ tsp. red wine vinegar

Whole wheat rolls

Directions:

Rehydrate the onions in a bowl or cup with the reserved beef liquid for 15 minutes. Drain.Heat oil in pan and sauté onions 2 minutes Add all ingredients except the beef and rolls. Bring to a boil, turn down heat and simmer 15 minutes. Shred the beef chunks and add to the sauce. Cook 5 minutes more. Serve on rolls. Makes 4 sandwiches.

## Chili Mac (Gayle)

Ingredients:

1 lb. freeze dried or canned hamburger

1 pint tomatoes

1 can red beans (or 1 cup cooked beans)

1 can tomato soup (or magic mix with tomato powder)

1 Tbs. dehydrated onion

1 Tbs. dehydrated green pepper

1 Tbs. dehydrated celery

1 Tbs. brown sugar

1 cup elbow macaroni

1 Tbs. Chili seasoning

Directions:

Reconstitute the freeze dried beef, if necessary. Place meat in skillet and heat. When meat is ready, add tomatoes, magic mix with tomato powder and beans. (See Chapter 3 for Magic Mix recipe.) Stir in onion, pepper and celery and brown sugar. Add cooked macaroni. Add taco seasoning.

# Beef Macaroni Skillet (Lynn)

Ingredients:

1 pint canned hamburger (or 1 lb. ground beef)

1 medium onion (or 1 Tablespoon instant minced onion)

3 cups tomato juice

1 Tbs. Worcestershire sauce

1 Tbs. vinegar

Salt and pepper to taste

1 tsp. dry mustard

1 cup uncooked elbow macaroni

Directions:

Place onion and contents of pint jar cooked ground beef in 12-inch skillet (or brown beef and onion in 12-inch skillet) and cook over medium heat. Add tomato juice, Worcestershire sauce, vinegar, salt, pepper, mustard, and macaroni. Bring to boil; reduce heat. Cover and simmer 20 minutes or until macaroni is tender. Stir occasionally during cooking.

# Corned Beef Hash (Gayle)

Ingredients:

2 cans corned beef

3 Tbs. canola oil

5 cups beef broth (or 5 cups water and 2 beef bullion cubes)

2 cups dehydrated diced potatoes

½ cup dehydrated onion

¼ cup powdered milk

Salt and pepper to taste

Directions:

In a pot, combine potatoes, onions, milk powder, beef broth and salt and pepper. Boil for 10 minutes or until beef broth is mostly absorbed. In a skillet, heat oil and add hydrated potatoes. Add corned beef. Cook another 20 minutes or until potatoes are browned, flipping contents frequently.

## Sweet and Sour Ham (Schatzie Ohio)

Ingredients:

1 can ham, canned chicken or spam

1 can pineapple tidbits

2 Tbs. oil

2 tsp. onion

2 tsp. green pepper

½ cup pineapple-apricot jam (or grape jelly)

½ cup ketchup

1 cup rice

Directions:

In a little oil sauté some onion, some fresh or reconstituted dry green pepper add the chunked ham and a can of drained pineapple tidbits. To make the sweet and sour sauce, mix equal portions of pineapple-apricot jam and ketchup. (This can also be made with grape jelly and ketchup.) Stir the sweet and sour sauce into the ham and pineapple mix and heat through. Serve with rice.

# Chicken Alfredo (Bitsy)

Ingredients:

     2/3 cup Magic Mix

     1 cup water

     1 cup parmesan cheese

     ½ tsp. of garlic

     ½ tsp. onion powder

     1 pint chicken

     1 lb. pasta

Directions:

Combine Magic Mix and water. (See Chapter 3 for Magic Mix recipe.) Whisk constantly over medium heat until sauce thickens. Turn down heat to low. Add chicken and warm through. Add cheese and seasonings. Stir until smooth. Serve over cooked pasta.

## Chicken Pot Pie Topped with Biscuits (Bitsy)

Ingredients:

1 pint chicken

2 tbs. celery

2 tbs. onion

½ tbs. garlic

1 T. chicken gravy powder

Magic Mix

½ cup milk

½ cup dehydrated potato disks

1 can peas and carrots

Biscuits

Directions:

In skillet, mix chicken with celery and onion. In separate bowl, combine gravy powder, magic mix, and milk. Wisk until blended. Add to skillet. Stir in rehydrated potato disks and peas and carrots. Add garlic. Cook until warmed through. Top with biscuit mix. (See Chapter 3 for biscuit recipe.) Cook for another 10 minutes or until biscuits are done.

# Chicken and Dressing (Vienna (Soggy Prepper))

Ingredients:

1 Tbs. oil

1 lb cooked chicken   (fresh cooked, canned, reconstituted dried)

1 box stuffing mix  (or make stuffing from old homemade bread)

1 can cream of mushroom (or magic mix with mushrooms)

1 can cream of chicken

1 onion   (or 1/2 cup dried, reconstituted)

2 stalks celery   (or 1/4 cup dried, reconstituted)

5 cups water

Directions:

In skillet, warm oil and toss in chicken, onion and celery and sauté a couple minutes. Dump in soups with about 4-5 cans water.  When it starts to simmer add in stuffing.

## Chipped Beef and Gravy (Bitsy)

Ingredients:

　　1 can chipped beef

　　2-3 Tbs. flour

　　Dry milk mixed to make 3 cups of liquid milk

Directions:

Tear beef into pieces about the size of a quarter. Fry over medium heat in non-stick skillet or seasoned cast iron until meat's edges curl a bit. Stir in flour until it coats meat. Turn down heat to low, immediately add milk, and stir constantly until milk thickens into gravy.

This can be served over toast, pancakes, potatoes, rice, biscuits, whatever starch you want. This is an excellent recipe to use up stale bread.

# Meat and Bean Gravy (LurkerBob)

Ingredients:

> 1lb hamburger (or any other chopped meat)
>
> 1 cup of mashed pinto beans
>
> 2 Tbs. dehydrated onions
>
> 1 can veggies (corn, carrots, mixed veggies, green beans)

Reconstitute the freeze dried beef (chicken or pork), if necessary. Place meat in skillet and heat. If using canned beef, reserve 2 tsp. liquid. If using fresh meat, reserve 2 tsp. drippings. Add one cup cooked mashed pinto beans. (This may be increased to 1½ cups to extend the meat.)

Gravy recipe

> 2 Tbs. flour
>
> 1 Tbs. cornstarch
>
> 1 ½ cup cold water
>
> 2 Tbs. drippings (if using fresh meats)

Add gravy. Recipe below. Add onions and the can of veggies. Stirring constantly, bring pan to a slow boil. Simmer for 20 minutes.

Serve over a starch (potatoes, noodles or rice).

## Biscuits and Gravy (Gayle)

Ingredients:

1 pint sausage (Tennessee Williams Country Sausage works well)

3 Tbs. bacon grease or shortening

¼ cup all purpose flour

3 cups liquid milk

salt and pepper to taste

Directions:

Prepare biscuits according to recipe in Chapter 3. Keep in warm oven until gravy is ready. Cook sausage in bacon grease. Do not drain grease. Add flour, salt and pepper. Cook until flour begins to brown. Then slowly add milk, stirring constantly. Simmer on low until gravy reaches desired thickness—about a minute or so. Slice biscuits in half and serve with warm gravy.

# Quinoa Salad (Breadmomma)

Ingredients:

1 cup quinoa

1 can black bean (or 1 cup prepared)

1 cup corn, rehydrated

2 oz red bell peppers, rehydrated

2 oz. red onion slices, rehydrated

1 Tbs. garlic

2 Tbs. vinegar or lemon juice

6 Tbs olive oil

Salt and pepper to taste

Directions:

Cook quinoa according to package directions. Add remaining ingredients and stir.

## Hot German Potato Salad (Schatzie Ohio)

Ingredients:

1 onion (or 1/4 cup minced onion)

1 Tbs. bacon fat

2 tablespoons sugar

2 teaspoons salt

1/4 teaspoon pepper

1/3 cup vinegar

1/4 cup water

6 red potatoes, cooked, peeled and sliced (or 6 cups dehydrated potato slices)

6 slices bacon, cooked and crumbled (or 1 can real bacon bits)

Directions:

In a large pan, fry onion in bacon fat. Add water, vinegar, sugar, salt and pepper. Cook until boiling. Add potatoes, stirring well. Serve hot.

# Coconut Curry Chicken (Veee)

Ingredients:

1 1/2 cup rice

1 Tbs. oil

2 tsp. curry powder

1 can (13.5 oz) coconut milk

1 can chicken

2 tsp. five-spice powder

Directions:

Prepare rice according to package directions. Warm oil in skillet. Add curry powder and cook for one minute. Add coconut milk and cook until reduced by half (about 7 minutes). Drain chicken and add to a bowl with the 5-spice. (See Chapter 8 for spice mix recipe.) Coat chicken. Add chicken to skillet and sauté for a few minutes. Serve over rice.

# Oriental Chicken Fried Rice (Veee)

Ingredients:

   1/4 cup oil

   2 cup cooked rice, cooled

   1/2 cup rehydrated dry onions (1-2 T dry)

   1 cup rehydrated shredded carrots (6-8 T dry)

   1/2 cup chopped chicken or 2 small cans drained

   1 Tbs.  peanut butter

   1/4 cup rehydrated peas, (1 T FD or dry)

   2 Tbs. soy sauce

   2 eggs (equivalent rehydrated powder)

   ½ tsp. garlic

   ¼ tsp. turmeric

   ½ tsp. cayenne or chili powder

Directions:

In large heavy frying pan, heat oil. Add rice, onion, chicken, and carrots. Stir frequently until rice begins to lightly brown. Add peanut butter, soy sauce, peas, and spices. Continue stirring while flavors mix. As rice mixture appears to be done, quickly add beaten egg mixture and continue stirring until egg is cooked. Serve at once with soy sauce, sweet and sour sauce, or hot mustard sauce.

# Risotto with Peas, Lemon Zest, and Tarragon (Veee)

Ingredients:

1-1/2 tsp. oil

1 cup Arborio rice (or short grained rice)

1/4 cup dry white wine

1 Tbs. dried onion

1/8 tsp. lemon peel, dried

1/4 tsp. tarragon, crushed

2 cups water

2 tsp. chicken bouillon

3/4 reconstituted peas

1/4 c grated Parmesan cheese

Salt and pepper to taste

Directions:

Heat oil over medium heat. Add rice and cook, stirring constantly, for 2 minutes. Add the wine and cook, stirring gently until the liquid is absorbed. Add the onion and other spices. Stir in the water and bouillon and cook, stirring occasionally. It should take about 25 minutes for all the broth to be absorbed. Remove from heat and stir in the peas, Parmesan cheese, salt and pepper.

# Tuna Rotini (Gayle)

Ingredients:

2 cans tuna

3 cups rotini

1 cup Italian dressing

1 pint corn relish (optional)

Any vegetables (optional)

Directions:

Cook rotini (or any noodles), drain and rinse under cool water. Add tuna and Italian dressing. Add diced veggies. (I add red onion, celery green pepper, yellow squash, tomato and cucumber.) If there are no fresh veggies available, add capers and olives. Add corn relish, if desired. Mix and serve chilled. If too dry, add more Italian dressing.

# Fettuccini with Capers, Olives and Tomatoes (UT Mom)

Ingredients:

1 Tbs. olive oil

¾ Tbs. minced dried garlic

2 Tbs. dried onion

2 cans (14.5 each) stewed tomatoes

2 Tbs. capers

1 can (15 oz) black olives, drained and halved

1 Tbs. Italian seasoning

½ Tbs. dried oregano

½ t red pepper flakes

½ t salt

1 8-oz pkg. fettuccini

½ cup grated Parmesan cheese

Directions:

Heat oil in a pot. Add garlic and onion, sauté for 1 minute. Lower heat to medium and add tomatoes (with their juice,) capers, olives, seasoning, red pepper, salt and oregano. Simmer for 30 minutes.

In another large pot, boil salted water, add fettuccini and cook al dente. Drain. Add fettuccini to sauce and mix well. Sprinkle with Parmesan cheese. Makes 4-5 servings. Spicy and good!

# Tuna Casserole (Gayle)

Ingredients:

2 cans tuna

1 can cream of mushroom soup (or magic mix with freeze dried mushrooms)

3 cups Egg Noodles

½ cup Parmesan cheese

Salt and pepper to taste

Directions:

Cook noodles, rinse and drain. Add magic mix with mushrooms (or use a can of cream of mushroom soup), and two cans of tuna. Mix well. Sprinkle cheese on top. Bake for 20 minutes at 350 degrees.

# Tuna Shells with Capers in White Wine Sauce (Veee)

Ingredients:

1 cup mini shells pasta

1 Tbs. oil

1 1/2 tsp. onion flakes

1 pinch red chili pepper flakes

1 can white chunk tuna, drained

1 Tbs. capers, drained (or 1 tsp. dried and reconstituted)

1/4 tsp salt

1 Tbs. dried parsley

1/4 cup white wine or chicken stock or water

Directions:

Cook pasta al dente and drain. While the pasta is cooking, prepare the rest of the recipe. In a sauté pan, heat oil on medium heat. Add dried chopped onion, pepper flakes, tuna, capers, salt, and parsley. Add wine and bring to simmer, and then lower heat to low. Cook for 10 minutes or longer, while the pasta cooks. If the mixture begins to dry out, add a little more wine or pasta water.

Add pasta to pan with tuna. Toss to mix. Add a few grinds of black pepper to taste.

# Linguine with Tuna, Walnuts, Lemon, and Herbs (Veee)

Ingredients:

1/2 lbs linguine

3 Tbs. walnuts, chopped

1 Tbs. oil

1 can tuna

2 tsp. lemon peel, dried

1/4 tsp. salt

1/4 tsp. pepper

1/4 tsp. garlic powder

1 tsp. dried parsley

1/8 tsp. thyme

1/4 tsp. dried chives

1 tsp. lemon juice

Directions:

Cook pasta until just done, about 12 minutes. Drain. In small frying pan, toast the walnuts over moderately low heat, stirring frequently, until golden brown, about 5 minutes. Or toast them in a 350 over for 5-10 minutes.

Meanwhile, in large frying pan, heat oil over moderate heat. Add lemon peel and all other spices, cook while stirring constantly for 1 minute or until fragrant. Stir in the tuna and break up the tuna with a fork. Remove from the heat. Toss the linguine with the tuna mixture, lemon juice, and the toasted walnuts.

# Linguine with Creamy Clam Sauce (Veee)

Ingredients:

1/2 lbs linguine

1 can Whole Clams, drained, reserve liquid

1/4 cup milk powder, reconstituted

3/4 cup water

1 Tbs. oil

1 Tbs. all purpose flour

1 tsp. dried chopped onion

1/4 tsp. garlic powder

1/2 tsp. dried basil, crushed

1/2 tsp. dried oregano, crushed

1/2 tsp. dried parsley

Salt and pepper to taste

2 Tbs. dry white wine

2 Tbs. grated Parmesan cheese

Directions:

Cook pasta uncovered al dente. Drain. Drain clams, reserving liquid. Add instant milk and water to reserved liquid to make 3/4 cup. In medium saucepan, warm oil. Stir in the flour, chopped onion, spices. Add milk mixture all at once. Cook on medium, stirring constantly until sauce is thick and bubbly. Cook and stir for 1 minute more. Stir in the wine and clams. Heat through. Serve sauce over hot pasta. Sprinkle with Parmesan cheese. Serve immediately.

# Salmon Patties (Gayle)

Ingredients:

1 can salmon

2 Tbs. egg powder, reconstituted

¼ cup potato flakes

1 Tbs. dehydrated onion

1 tsp. garlic flakes

¼ tsp. dill

¼ tsp. celery salt

2 Tbs. oil

Directions:

Combine ingredients (except olive oil) in a medium bowl and form into patties about a half inch thick. Heat oil in pan and cook patties for about five minutes on each side. Serve with mashed potatoes and green beans.

# CHAPTER 7: DESSERTS

# Flaky Pie Crust (Repair Momma)

*Yield: 2 crusts*

Ingredients

2 2/3 cups sifted regular all-purpose flour

1 tsp. salt

1 cup shortening

6 Tbs. ice-cold water

Directions:

Combine flour, salt and shortening in large mixing bowl. Cut well with pastry cutter. Add ice-cold water. Cut with pastry cutter, thoroughly. (Always cut never stir.) Dampen counter with wet cloth and lay plastic wrap down. Sprinkle wrap with flour. Divide in half. Shape into balls. Roll out on floured saran wrap, adding flour (sifted) as needed to keep from sticking. Carefully slide hand under plastic wrap. Invert pie plate over top of pie crust, center it and flip it into position; peel plastic wrap carefully off. Trim edges and shape as desired.

See Chapter 5 for pie filling recipes. To make a pie, prepare bottom crust as outlined above. Dump in a quart pie filling. Add top crust and make vent holes. Place in oven and bake for 40 minutes at 425 degrees.

# Peach Cobbler (Kate from Ga.)

Ingredients:

2 pints peaches (or two large cans)

1 1/2 cups whole wheat flour

1 cup sugar

3 Tbs. cornstarch

1 1/2 tsp baking powder

1/2 tsp. salt

1 1/2 cups milk

½ tsp. cinnamon (optional)

Directions:

Grease a 9 x 11 glass baking dish. Mix sugar, flour, baking powder, salt, cornstarch together. Add the milk a little at a time. You don't want it to form lumps. Pour in baking dish. Gently spoon peaches on top.

After you spoon the peaches on top, gently pour the syrup from cans on top of everything. Sometimes I use the syrup from both cans and sometimes I only use one. If two cans of syrup looks like too much then only try one the first time you make it. Sprinkle on the cinnamon and bake at 350 degrees for 30 to 45 minutes.

# Chocolate Cake (Winnabird)

Ingredients:

1 1/4 cups all-purpose flour

2 cups sugar

1 cup unsweetened cocoa powder

2 tsp. baking soda

1/2 tsp. salt

1 1/2 tsp. vanilla extract

2/3 cup vegetable oil (or melted shortening)

2 tsp. white vinegar (or lemon juice)

2 cups cold water

Directions:

Preheat oven to 350F. Grease and flour two 8 inch or 9 inch round cake pans (or makes 24 cupcakes). Set aside.

Sift the dry ingredients together. Set aside.

Mix vanilla extract, oil, vinegar and cold water. Slowly whisk the wet ingredients into the dry ingredients, being careful not to over mix. Mixture will be quite wet but that is OK.

Pour batter into the prepared pans and bake until a tester inserted in the center comes out clean--about 30 minutes. For cupcakes, the baking time is 24 to 26 minutes.

Cool in the pans for 10 minutes, then invert onto a wire rack to cool.

# Butter Recipe Yellow Cake

Ingredients:

    2 cups flour

    1 Tbs. baking powder

    2 Tbs. egg powder

    1 Tbs. butter powder

    1 tsp. salt

    1 ¾ cup water

    1 ½ cup white sugar

    ½ cup oil or melted shortening

    1 tsp. vanilla

Directions:

Preheat oven to 350F. Grease and flour two 8 inch or 9 inch round cake pansSet aside.

Sift the dry ingredients together.  Set aside.

Mix water, sugar, oil and vanilla. Slowly whisk the wet ingredients into the dry ingredients, being careful not to over mix.

Pour batter into the prepared pans and bake until a tester inserted in the center comes out clean--about 25-30 minutes.

Cool in the pans for 10 minutes, then invert onto a wire rack to cool.

# Hot Fudge Frosting

3 cups sugar

1 cup cocoa powder

½ tsp. salt

½ cup cornstarch

4 Tbs. butter powder, reconstituted

1 cup liquid milk

2 tsp. vanilla

Directions:

Combine all ingredients except vanilla in medium saucepan. Cook until thickened, stirring constantly. Remove from heat and add vanilla. Spread warm frosting on cooled cake. (Hint: To make the cake easier to frost, combine ¼ cup white sugar dissolved in ½ cup water. Brush on cake. Let dry.)

# Applesauce Cake (Repair Momma)

Ingredients:

    2 cups all-purpose flour

    1 tsp. baking soda

    1 tsp. ground cinnamon

    1/4 tsp. ground cloves

    1/2 cup raisins

    1/2 cup chopped nuts

    1/2 cup shortening (or reconstituted butter)

    1 cup granulated sugar

    1 cup applesauce

Directions:

Preheat oven to 350°F. Grease and flour an 8-inch square baking pan; set aside.

Combine flour, baking soda, cinnamon, cloves, nuts and raisins in a medium bowl; set aside.

Mix shortening (or butter, if using) into sugar. Add applesauce; beat well. Stir in flour mixture. Pour batter into prepared baking pan. Bake for 40 minutes, or until tested done when a wooden pick inserted in center comes out clean. Serve warm.

# Pineapple Upside Down Cake (Kate from Georgia)

Ingredients

1 can crushed pineapple

1 cup brown sugar

1 cup all purpose flour

2 tsp. baking powder

2 Tbs. egg powder

¼ cup white sugar

½ tsp. salt

½ cup milk powder, reconstituted

1 tsp. vanilla

¼ cup melted shortening

Directions:

Grease 9 x 12 glass baking dish.

Pour pineapple into baking dish. Sprinkle with brown sugar.

In medium bowl, combine reconstituted milk, vanilla and shortening. Set aside.

In a separate bowl, combine flour, baking powder, egg powder, sugars and salt. Add dry ingredients to wet ingredients and mix until blended.

Pour batter over pineapple-brown sugar mixture.

Bake for 30 minutes at 350 degrees.

# Lemon Pound Cake (Gayle)

Ingredients:

    1/2 cup liquid milk

    ½ tsp. lemon juice

    1 cup white sugar

    ½ cup butter, reconstituted

    3 Tbs. reconstituted egg powder, divided

    ½ tsp. vanilla

    ¼ tsp. salt

    ½ tsp. baking soda

    1 cup and 1 Tbs. flour

Directions:

Reconstitute milk powder to make 1/2 cup of liquid milk. Add lemon juice. Let sit five minutes. In a separate bowl, combine sugar, butter and half of the reconstituted egg. Add soured milk, vanilla and remaining eggs. Add salt, baking soda and flour. Mix well and pour into greased loaf pan. Bake for one hour at 350 degrees.

# Lemon Glaze

Ingredients:

    2 cups powdered sugar

    1 Tbs. milk powder

    1 Tbs. water

    2 Tbs. lemon juice

Directions:

Combine ingredients and mix well. If necessary, add 1-2 tsp. water to get proper icing consistency. Pour over cake once cake has cooled.

# Oatmeal Raisin Cookies (Nancy)

Ingredients:

1 cup shortening

1 cup sugar

1 cup brown sugar

2 Tbs. egg powder, reconstituted

1 tsp. vanilla

2 cups flour

2 cups oatmeal

½ tsp. salt

2 tsp. baking powder

2 tsp. baking soda

1 cup raisins

Directions:

In a large bowl combine shortening, sugars and reconstituted egg powder. Mix in vanilla. Set aside.

In a small bowl, mix flour, oatmeal, salt, baking powder, baking soda. Add to large bowl. Mix well. Add chocolate chips, if using. Mix well.

Drop onto greased cookie sheet and bake for 12 minutes at 350 degrees.

Variations: Add 1 cup of any of the following: chocolate chips, walnuts, peacans, or coconut.

# Chocolate Chip Cookies (Nancy)

Ingredients:

      1 cup shortening

      1 Tbs. butter powder

      ¾ cup white sugar

      ¾ cup brown sugar

      2 eggs, reconstituted

      1 tsp. vanilla extract

      2 ¼ cup flour

      1 tsp. baking soda

      ½ tsp. salt

      1 pkg. chocolate chips

Directions:

Preheat oven to 350 degrees.

In medium bowl, cream shortening, butter powder, sugars, reconstituted egg and vanilla. Set aside.

In a separate bowl, mix flour, baking soda and salt. Add dry ingredients to wet ingredients.

Stir. Mix in chocolate chips.

Bake for 10-12 minutes at 350 degrees.

# Apple Cinnamon Cookies (Gayle)

Ingredients:

  1 cup diced apple, reconstituted

  1 cup shortening

  1 cup honey

  2 Tbs. egg powder

  ½ cup liquid milk

  3 ½ cups flour

  1 Tbs. butter powder

  2 tsp. baking powder

  ¾ tsp. baking soda

  ½ tsp. salt

  ½ tsp. cinnamon

Directions:

Preheat oven to 375 degrees.

Prepare one cup reconstituted apple pieces. Set aside.

Cream shortening and honey. Slowly add reconstituted egg and reconstituted milk, mixing as you go. Add reconstituted apples. Mix.

In a separate bowl, sift flour, butter powder, baking powder, baking soda, salt and cinnamon. Add dry ingredients to wet ingredients.

Drop onto greased cookie sheet. Bake for 12-15 minutes at 375 degrees.

**Peanut Butter Cookies (Gayle)**

Ingredients:

1 ½ cup peanut butter

1/3 cup shortening

½ cup white sugar

½ cup brown sugar

1 tsp. vanilla

3 Tbs. egg powder, reconstituted

1 ¼ cup flour

½ tsp. baking powder

2 ½ tsp. baking soda

½ tsp. salt

Directions:

Cream peanut butter, sugars and vanilla. Set aside.

In a separate bowl, combine egg powder, flour, baking powder, baking soda and salt. Mix. Slowly pour dry ingredients into peanut butter blend. Mix until blended.

Roll into 2 inch balls and place on ungreased cookie sheet. Mash with a fork in a crisscross pattern. Bake for 10 to 12 minutes at 350 degrees.

**Five Minute Fudge Candy Bars (Hunker-Down)**

Ingredients:

1 lb. almond bark

12 oz. pkg. semi-sweet chocolate chips

1 cup (or more) peanuts

Directions:

Combine almond bark and chocolate chips in a crock pot. As soon as possible, stir in the nuts. We prefer to keep pouring in as many nuts as possible, as long as they are coated with the chocolate. Do not allow the heat to get high enough to crystallize the sugar. Drop tablespoon size portions on waxed paper to chill.

We use the microwave instead of a crock pot, it's much faster. Microwave the almond bark and chocolate chips on high for 3 minutes. Do not exceed 3 minutes or the sugar will crystallize. Remove from microwave and stir in the nuts. Drop tablespoon size portions on waxed paper to chill.

Storage method: Vacuum seal and place in freezer.

Storage time: Both the almond bark and chocolate chip makers have a use by date of 18 months. We add one year to that number to offset the manufactures need to obsolete their product ASAP. We add another year because we store
the bars in the freezer. It would be great if storage life was 5-10 years but we limit our estimated expiration date to 3.5 years because of the oil present in every ingredient. Our 3 to 5 year estimate has not been tested.

# Homemade Gelatin (Judy, Another One)

Ingredients:

2 envelopes of unflavored gelatin like Knox

1 cup water or juice (I like the juice the best)

1 cup boiling water

1 cup sugar

1 envelope of unsweetened powdered drink mix (Kool-aid) any flavor

Directions:

Put the cup of cold water in a heat-proof bowl and sprinkle the gelatin over the water. Whisk until combined and let set 5 minutes to soften. Add boiling water, sugar and drink mix. Whisk until no granules remain. Refrigerate until firm.

## Sport Electrolyte Drink Mix (Judy, Another One)

Ingredients:

10 Tbs. sugar OR 1/3 cup sugar plus 1/4 tsp stevia

1/4 tsp. No-salt

1/2 tsp. salt

1 package unsweetened drink mix (kool-aid)

Directions:

Mix the powders together then add to 2 quarts of water. Mix well and chill.

## Horchata de Arroz (Ron)

Ingredients:

      2 cups water, divided

      1 cup rice, cooked

      1/2 cinnamon stick

      1/4 cup sweetened condensed milk

      1/2 cup sugar

      1/8 tsp. vanilla

Directions:

Mix 1 cup water, rice and cinnamon stick and let sit for an hour. Then add remaining cup of water, condensed milk, sugar and vanilla. Pour mixture into blender and blend. Strain out bits of rice. Serve chilled.

# CHAPTER 8: SPICE MIXES,
## SAUCES, DRESSINGS AND MARINADES

# SPICE MIXES

## Pulled Pork Spice Mix (Veee)

Ingredients:

4 Tbs. paprika

2 Tbs. chili powder, cumin, brown sugar, salt

1 Tbs. pepper, oregano, sugar, white pepper, garlic powder, onion powder,

1 Tbs. cayenne pepper (optional)

Directions:

Mix ingredients and store in airtight container.

# Curry Powder (TG)

Ingredients:

8 Tbs. cumin

7 Tbs. coriander

2 Tbs. ginger

4 Tbs. tumeric

1/2 Tbs. cayenne or chili powder.

Directions:

Mix ingredients and store in airtight container.

# Apple Pie Spice (TG)

Ingredients:

      1/2 tsp. cinnamon

      1/4 tsp. nutmeg

      1/8 tsp. allspice

      1/8 tsp. ground cardamom

Directions:

Mix ingredients and store in airtight container.

# Pumpkin Pie Spice

Ingredients:

    1 tsp. ground cinnamon

    1/4 tsp. ground nutmeg

    1/4 tsp. ground ginger

    1/8 tsp. ground cloves

Directions:

Mix ingredients and store in airtight container.

# Allspice Substitute (TG)

Ingredients:

1/2 tsp. cinnamon

1/2 tsp. ground cloves

1/2 tsp. nutmeg

Directions:

Mix ingredients and store in airtight container.

**Seasoned Salt (TG)**

Ingredients:

6 Tbs. salt

1/2 tsp. dried thyme

1/2 tsp. dried marjoram

1/2 tsp. garlic powder

2 1/4 tsp. paprika

1 tsp. dried mustard

1/4 tsp. onion powder

1/8 tsp. dried dill

1/2 tsp. celery salt

Directions:

Mix ingredients and store in airtight container.

# Taco Seasoning Mix (TG)

Ingredients:

1 Tbs. chili powder

1/4 tsp. garlic powder

1/4 tsp. onion powder

1/4 tsp. crushed red pepper flakes

1/4 tsp. dried oregano

1/2 tsp. paprika

1 1/2 ground cumin

1 tsp. salt

1 tsp. black pepper

Directions:

Mix ingredients and store in airtight container.

# Cajun Mix (Gayle)

Ingredients:

1/4 cup salt

1/4 cup cayenne pepper

2 Tbs. ground white pepper

2 Tbs. ground black pepper

2 Tbs. paprika

2 Tbs. onion powder

2 Tbs. garlic powder

2 Tbs. cumin

2 Tbs. paprika

Directions:

Mix ingredients and store in airtight container.

# Mild Cajun Mix (TG)

Ingredients:

    2 tsp. salt

    2 tsp. garlic powder

    2 1/2 tsp. paprika

    1 tsp. black pepper

    1 tsp. onion powder

    1 tsp. cayenne pepper

    1 1/4 tsp. dried oregano

    1/2 tsp. red pepper flakes

Directions:

Mix ingredients and store in airtight container.

# Dry Onion Mix (TG)

Ingredients:

       4 Tbs. beef bullion granules

       3 Tbs. dehydrated onion

       1 tsp. onion powder

       ¼ tsp. salt

       1/8 tsp. pepper

Directions:

Mix ingredients and store in airtight container.

# DESSERT SAUCES

## Chocolate Syrup (TG)

Ingredients:

       1 1/2 cups water

       1 1/2 cups sugar

       1 cup cocoa powder

       Dash of salt

       1 tsp. vanilla

Directions:

Mix everything except vanilla together in a saucepan. Over medium heat bring it to a simmer, stirring constantly. Remove from heat, stir in vanilla. Use immediately or store in the fridge.

# Carmel Sauce (Kate in Georgia)

Ingredients:

1/2 cup butter powder

1 1/2 cups sugar

2 Tbs. corn syrup

2 tsp. vanilla

3/4 cup buttermilk (use powdered – then reconstitute.)

Directions:

I also add a bit extra water to get the correct consistency. However, if you reconstitute the butter powder that won't be necessary. I never bother to reconstitute anything; I just use extra water if necessary.

Place all ingredients except vanilla in an extra large saucepan. (This will create a LOT of foam so be sure to use a big pan.) Bring to a boil and cook for 7 minutes. Stir constantly to prevent scorching. Remove from heat and add vanilla extract.

# Butterscotch Sauce (TG)

Ingredients:

2 cans sweetened condensed milk

2 packages (11 oz each) butterscotch chips

2 Tbs. vinegar

1 Tbs. ground cinnamon

Directions:

In heavy saucepan combine ingredients. Cook over low heat stirring constantly until smooth.

# SALAD DRESSING

## Italian Dressing

Ingredients:

2 tsp. garlic powder

¼ tsp. salt

1/8 tsp. pepper

¼ tsp. white sugar

½ tsp. oregano

1/8 tsp. paprika

1/8 tsp. basil

1/8 tsp. marjoram

¾ cup olive oil

½ cup red wine vinegar

Directions:

Mix ingredients and shake before serving. Store extra salad dressing in refrigerator.

# Ranch Dressing

Ingredients:

 1/8 tsp. garlic powder

 2 tsp. minced onion

 2 tsp. parsley

 ½ tsp. salt

 1/8 tsp. pepper

 1 cup mayonnaise

 1 cup buttermilk (or 1 cup reconstituted milk and 1 Tbs. lemon juice)

Directions:

Mix ingredients and shake before serving. Store extra salad dressing in refrigerator.

# French Dressing

Ingredients:

       1 tsp. dry mustard

       1/8 tsp. onion powder

       1 ½ tsp. paprika

       1 tsp. salt

       ¼ cup sugar

       ¼ cup vinegar

       ¾ cup olive oil

Directions:

Mix ingredients and shake before serving. Store extra salad dressing in refrigerator.

# MARINADES

## Teriyaki Sauce (TG)

Ingredients:

       1/4 cup vegetable oil

       1/4 cup soy sauce

       2 Tbs. catsup

       1 Tbs. red wine vinegar

       2 cloves garlic crushed

       1/4 tsp. pepper

Directions:

Combine all ingredients and stir well. Recipe can be doubled or tripled, and contents stored in the refrigerator.

## Korean Marinade (AZ Rookie Prepper)

Ingredients:

       3 Tbs. chopped garlic (about 2 cloves)

       3 Tbs. soy sauce

       2 Tbs. sugar

       1 Tbs. honey

       2 Tbs. fresh squeezed juice from an Asian pear (or juice from canned pears)

       1 Tbs. Japanese rice wine (or dry white wine)

       1 Tbs. sesame oil

       3 green onions, finely chopped (can dehydrated onion)

       1 tsp. pepper

Directions:

Mix marinade together until sugar and honey is dissolved. Marinade can be stored in refrigerator or freezer. Marinade for use on beef, pork, and chicken.

**Sesame Ginger Marinade (Gayle)**

Ingredients:

½ cup soy sauce

1/3 cup rice wine vinegar

1/3 cup canola oil

1/3 cup sesame oil

3 Tbs. honey

2 Tbs. minced ginger

1 Tbs. minced garlic

## Italian Spicy Dry Rub Seasoning (AZ Rookie Prepper)

Ingredients:

      1 packet Italian seasoning

      1/4 teaspoon cayenne pepper

      Pinch of rosemary (finely chopped or use a mortar and pestle)

      Pinch of thyme (finely chopped or use a mortar and pestle)

Directions:

Mix together all ingredients. Rub into meat (works on beef, pork, chicken, pretty much any type meat). Let it marinate for at least 30 minutes, 1 hour is better. Grill meat.

## Sweet Kansas City Style BBQ Sauce (AZ Rookie Prepper)

Ingredients:

1 cup ketchup

1/4 cup water

1/4 cup apple cider vinegar

1/4 cup brown sugar

3 Tbs. chili powder

2 tsp. pickled garlic, minced

1 tsp. cayenne

Directions:

Combine ingredients and simmer for 15-20 minutes until it gets thick.

Variations: Increase the vinegar (slightly) if you like bbq sauce that is thinner and vinegary. Add 1/4 teaspoon of liquid smoke if you want to add a smoky flavor. Add 1 tablespoon of onion powder and 2 tablespoons of mustard powder if you want tangy sauce without the heat. Add 1/3 cup brown sugar instead of ¼ cup if you like your bbq sauce sweeter. Add more or less chili powder and/or cayenne powder, depending on your tastes.

# White Wine Marinade (Mominem)

Ingredients

  1 cup soy sauce (low sodium is fine)

  1 cup vegetable or olive oil

  2 cups white wine or clear soft drink (Sprite or 7 Up)

  1 Tbs. garlic powder (or 3 cloves of garlic)

  1 Tbs. black pepper

Directions:

Marinate overnight and grill. Marinade works on chicken, turkey and foul.

## Guamanian Marinade (Ron on the Rio)

Ingredients:

1/2 cup soy sauce

1/2 cup brown sugar

1/2 cup pineapple juice

1/3 cup onion powder

Dash of garlic

Dash of white pepper

Directions:

Marinate ribs or chicken for 24 hours.

# Butt Rub (Mickey59)

Ingredients

1 cup brown sugar

3 tsp. salt

1 tsp. chili powder

3 tsp. sweet paprika

1/2 tsp. granulated garlic

1/2 tsp. onion powder

1/4 tsp. cayenne pepper

1/4 tsp. black pepper

1/4 tsp. dry mustard

1/4 tsp. celery salt

Directions:

Mix and store in a sealed container. If you make a triple batch, you can change all the teaspoon measurements to tablespoons. And of course, the brown sugar will then be 3 cups.

## APPENDIX A: SUBSTITUTIONS

| Ingredient | Amount | Substitute |
|---|---|---|
| Baking Powder | 1 tsp. | ¼ tsp. baking soda + ½ tsp. cream of tarter |
| Buttermilk | 1 Cup | 1 cup milk + 1 Tbs. lemon juice or vinegar (let sit for five minutes to sour) |
| Chocolate (unsweetened) | 1 Baker's Square | 3 Tbs cocoa + 1 Tbs. butter |
| Chocolate (semi-sweet) | 1 Baker's Square | 3 Tbs. cocoa + 1 Tbs. butter + 4 tsp. sugar |
| Cornstarch | 1 ½ Tbs. | 1 Tbs. Flour |
| Flour (all-purpose) | 1 Cup | 1 cup hard wheat<br><br>½ cup hard wheat + ½ cup soft wheat |
| Flour (bread) | 1 Cup | 1 cup all purpose flour + 1 Tbs. vital wheat gluten + 1/8 tsp. ascorbic acid |
| Flour (cake) | 1 Cup | 1 cup all purpose flour (minus 2 Tbs.) + 2 Tbs. cornstarch |
| Flour (self-rising) | 1 Cup | 1 cup cake flour + 1 tsp. baking powder + ½ tsp. salt |
| Flour (pastry) | 1 Cup | 1 cup soft wheat |
| Corn Syrup | 1 ½ Cup | 1 cup white sugar + 1 cup water<br><br>1 cup honey |
| Egg | 1 Egg | 1 tsp. unflavored gelatin + 3 Tbs. cold water + 2 ½ Tbs. boiling water |

|  |  | 1 Tbs. mayonnaise |
|  |  | 1 Tbs. dehydrated eggs + 2 Tbs. cold water |
| Milk | 1 Cup | ½ cup evaporated milk + ½ cup water |
|  |  | 1/3 cup milk powder + 1 cup water |
| Shortening | 1 Cup | 2/3 cup melted vegetable oil |

# APPENDIX B:

## EQUIVALENT MEASUREMENTS

**Tablespoons to Cups**

3 tsp. = 1 Tbs.

2 Tbs. = 1/8 cup

4 Tbs. = ¼ cup

8 Tbs. = ½ cup

16 Tbs. = 1 cup


**Ounces to Cups**

2 oz. = ¼ cup

 4 oz. = ½ cup

8 oz. = 1 cup


**Cups, Pints, Quarts, Gallons, Pecks and Bushels**

2 cups = 1 pint

2 pints = 1 quart

4 quarts = 1 gallon

2 gallons = 1 peck

4 pecks = 1 bushel

# RECPIE INDEX

## CHAPTER 2: BREADS

## CHAPTER 3: SOUPS

## CHAPTER 4: CANNING

## CHAPTER 5: BREAKFAST

## CHAPTER 6: DINNER

## CHAPTER 7: DESSERTS

## CHAPTER 8: SPICE MIXES, SAUCES, DRESSINGS AND MARINADES